In her thoughtful, grounded work, Purifoy [...] peacemaking, and how they often resembl[...] to shape and love places with all of ourselves and reveals [...] surprisingly—may be nourished and cared for in return, if we're willing.

Anne Bogel, creator of Modern Mrs Darcy and host of the What Should I Read Next podcast

Is there a special prize for the best books about home? If so, I want to give it to Christie Purifoy. If you appreciate beautiful stories about house and home and all the many ways places change us as we go about changing them, *Placemaker* is the book you've been waiting for.

Myquillyn Smith, author of *Cozy Minimalist Home* and *The Nesting Place*

Carl Rogers said, "What is most personal is most universal." I kept thinking of that while reading Christie Purifoy's smart and beautiful book, *Placemaker*. Page after page of the winding path that led her family to a place called Maplehurst caused me to reflect on my own life, the places I've sought to make, and how they in equal measure ended up making me.

John Blase, author of *The Jubilee: Poems*

In *Placemaker*, Christie Purifoy has given the world a deeply beautiful and profound work of art. Encircled here are stories of loss, grief, hope, and resurrection, that though rooted in both natural history and Christie's own history, make room for us and manage to transcend the earthly world. Here we are reminded that placemaking is a vocational invitation from God for all of us—regardless of where we live or how we make our way in the world. I will return often to this book, and know that with each reading, I will find new treasures to carry with me into the next season.

Kris Camealy, author of *Come, Lord Jesus: The Weight of Waiting*, and *Holey, Wholly, Holy: A Lenten Journey of Refinement*

In one sense, placemaking is a particular story rooted in a Pennsylvania farmhouse and shaded by the canopies of tall and aging trees. In another sense, it's the universal story, swept up and carried in the river of human longing: to belong. As Purifoy so lyrically illustrates, placemaking isn't just what we make of our places. It's the spiritual practice of naming, of knowing, of remembering.

Jen Pollock Michel, award-winning author of *Teach Us to Want, Keeping Place*, and *Surprised by Paradox*

Christie's words are lyrical beauty, an ode to place and peace. This book is a gentle call to all, no matter where God has us, to make place and cultivate hope.

Hannah Queen, author of *Honey and Jam*

Warning: this book will make you homesick—for people as well as for places. It also might make you wish for a green thumb. It will definitely move you toward your garden and your neighbors. Christie channels Madeleine L'Engle and Tasha Tudor in this love letter to the history of places and the people who have made their home in them. When you're done you might be tempted to put Maplehurst into your GPS, because some places just have to been seen in person. If Christie's words are anything to go by, I think it will be even better than you imagined.

Lisa-Jo Baker, author of *Never Unfriended* and co-host of the Out of the Ordinary Podcast

Placemaker

CULTIVATING PLACES *of* COMFORT, BEAUTY, AND PEACE

CHRISTIE PURIFOY

For my father, W.M. "Mark" Day

They will be called oaks of righteousness, a planting
of the Lord for the display of his splendor.

Isaiah 61:3

ZONDERVAN

Placemaker
Copyright © 2019 by Christie Purifoy

Requests for information should be addressed to:
Zondervan, *3900 Sparks Dr. SE, Grand Rapids, Michigan 49546*

ISBN 978-0-310-35224-2 (softcover)

ISBN 978-0-310-35225-9 (ebook)

Published in association with William K. Jensen Literary Agency, 119 Bampton Court, Eugene, Oregon 97404.

Cover design: James W. Hall IV
Cover illustration: Lindley Library, RHS, London, UK/Bridgeman Images
Interior design: Kait Lamphere

Printed in the United States of America

19 20 21 22 23 24 25 26 27 28 29 /LSC/ 15 14 13 12 11 10 9 8 7 6 5 4 3 2 1

Contents

Forests and Orchards

OUR INVITATION TO LIVE AS PLACEMAKERS

The first trees I ever loved graced the cover of my tattered paperback copy of *The Magician's Nephew*, one of the Chronicles of Narnia by C. S. Lewis. Those trees were stick-straight, and the forest they made together was as perfectly planted as an orchard. In that stylized image, there was no prickly undergrowth to grab a child's legs, no low-hanging branches to tangle in her hair, no fallen logs to block her way. There were simply a comforting green roof and the quiet spaces between the trees. For most of my life, I have felt the joy of recognition whenever I encounter a forest with little or no scrub. "It's a Narnian forest!" I say. But no one has ever understood what I mean by that, and they are right to be confused. The forest on the cover of this particular edition of the book is not an image of Narnia, but of a portal where a young boy named Digory and his friend Polly discover they can enter many worlds, some old and dying, some young and growing.

Recently, when I began to wonder how trees had come to mean so much to me, I went in search of that old book. When I found it, I was startled to realize that the forest of my memory was the background of a very different picture. In the foreground, a witch queen emerges from a blue pond, her fists grasped tightly around Polly's long blonde hair. Polly, meanwhile, is holding hands with Digory, and the two children seem to be magically flying up and out of the forest behind them. Somehow, I had forgotten all of the foreground drama and remembered only the perfect tranquility of those background trees. It seems I have always longed for a place of deeply rooted peace.

No gentle forests ever welcomed me in the landscapes of my Texas childhood. The nearest thing I encountered was the pecan orchard on my great-grandfather's farm. I recall seeing it only once. I noticed it through the glass window of our family station wagon as my father drove us, his four children, to visit his grandfather. I had never seen an orchard before, and I didn't understand at first what I was seeing. *How did these perfectly spaced trees come to be here in this flat, creek-bottom land?* Before I could voice the question, our station wagon lumbered up the dusty gravel road, leaving the creek and the trees behind. I figured it out later that year, around Christmastime, as I watched my father shell pecans from the paper sack he'd brought home from the family farm. *Ah*, I thought, *those pecan trees did not simply grow there by chance. They were planted.*

An orchard is not a forest, though. Most forests arise naturally over time, but an orchard is a collaboration—an intentional partnership between us and the creator-God in whose image we are made. Our God may have created the trees, like Aslan singing Narnian flora into being, but we continue that work when we study the climate and the soil and determine whether to cultivate pecan, apple, or pear. We plant seeds or saplings in neat rows. We prune limbs, and we tend the soil. We do not make the trees, but we make a place for them.

Like the God to whom we belong, we are placemakers.

In my lifetime, the media has rarely delivered good news, yet I struggle to recall a time when reports of politics and international affairs have left me feeling as desperate for a peaceful refuge as I have of late. When global and national arenas turn into battlegrounds, many of us instinctively retreat toward home. We trade the newspaper for a magazine featuring homemade comfort foods, we neglect serious websites in favor of home design and gardening blogs, and we scroll Instagram feeds devoted to farmhouses or cabins in the woods. If our hearts have been shaped by grace and faith, we bend beneath a heavy new burden of guilt. Aren't we meant to engage a hurting world rather than retreat to our own private Edens?

> *Making and tending good and beautiful places is not a dishonorable retreat. It is a holy pursuit.*

For more than twenty years, my husband Jonathan and I have learned to care for others by caring for the places in which they dwell. Creating and cultivating shelter has brought us happiness and heartache and more than a few unanswered questions, but there is one thing I know absolutely: making and tending good and beautiful places is not a dishonorable retreat. It is a holy pursuit. Our maker has made a home for us sheltered by trees, bounded by rivers, and illuminated by both stars and the white-blooming flowers of evening. Yet we were never meant merely to consume the gifts of creation. We were made to collaborate. We were made to participate. This book is an invitation to reconsider your own relationship to the ground beneath your feet and the roof over your head.

What will you find on the pages that follow? You will find portraits of the many places I have loved. You will find portraits of some of the flawed yet inspiring placemakers who shaped those places in the past. You will discover what these places reveal about the costs and the rewards of following a God who delights in places as well as people. From a brick farmhouse built by Pennsylvania Quakers to city windowsills where wheatgrass grows in recycled yogurt pots, from a scarred and stained kitchen table to a picnic spread beneath a shady silver maple, I hope my stories inspire you to set a table with care, pick up a hammer with courage, or plant a seed with hope. In these small yet deliberate ways, we can cultivate dwellings of peace for ourselves, for others, and for the glory of the One who first made us and placed us in a garden. We, too, can be placemakers. It is a worthwhile pursuit. Yet I cannot say that the placemaker's life is an easy life. I cannot promise that it will not break your heart.

Four years ago, I planted my first trees—all antique apple trees. Jonathan and I planted them during our first spring at Maplehurst, the Pennsylvania farmhouse we now call home. I chose the trees from a catalog of heritage apple varieties. I wish I could say I chose these varieties for the poetry of their names or the complexity of their flavor profiles, but the truth is more mundane. I was overwhelmed by the number of selections and simply ticked the box for a discounted shipment of four—one for each of our children. Fortunately, we did not explain the significance of the number to those same children. Two years later, the apple tree on the far end of the line failed to blossom when spring beckoned. A mouse or rabbit had eaten the bark at the base of the small trunk right around in a circle. The tree was "girdled." A wound like that is scarcely noticeable, but it is deadly, and our infant orchard decreased by one. The three remaining trees now give us apples every fall, though not many. And despite the fact that these trees are visible from the window over our kitchen sink, we do sometimes forget to pick the apples before they turn from ripe to rotten.

When did I realize that the idealized forest memory with such a hold on me was, in fact, an invitation? At some point, long before I planted my apple trees, I began deliberately to cultivate places where peace could dwell, and I have never regretted the costs of that commitment. Yet here at Maplehurst, my faith has faltered. Here, we have lost more than one small apple tree, and we have faced challenges as dense as any undergrowth that ever barred the way between the trees. On the pages that follow, I will bring my past to bear on my present. I will look for evidence of what I do still, deep down, believe: nature is singing a song, the trees are clapping their hands, and we are called to join them.[1] With God's help, we can pick up the pieces of an old and dying world, and we can make them new. We can make a place where beauty and peace can take root, flourish, and grow.

If peace is a state of harmony, if it is a kind of wholeness or completeness, then peaceful places are spacious places where our whole selves can abide. They are places with room enough for our joys and our sorrows, room enough for our neighbors and all those in need of comfort, rest, and renewal.

What is placemaking? It is deliberately sending your roots deep into a place, like a tree. It means allowing yourself to be nourished by a place even as you shape it for the better. It is creative work for men and women; it is possible whether you are employed outside your home or within it. Unlike hospitality, it is sometimes solitary and sometimes communal. It is work for introverts like myself and extroverts like my husband. Placemaking depends on rootedness, but it does not deny the realities of our contemporary, nomadic lives. We can be placemakers whether we are homebodies or world travelers. We can be placemakers whether we care for a farmhouse in the country or share a dorm room at a university. We can and should be placemakers whether we intend to stay or know we'll be moving on in six months.

With God's help, we can pick up the pieces of an old and dying world, and we can make them new. We can make a place where beauty and peace can take root, flourish, and grow.

I still believe in the placemaking life I have lived for so many years and in so many places, but the home I have found at Maplehurst seems determined to remake me even while I struggle to restore it. Questions I had long refused to hear have become more insistent. *If it is possible to cultivate places of peace, does that work endure, and does it bear lasting fruit? Can the work of our hands be established, or does decay eventually bring everything to ruin?* When the apple tree you planted with your own hands dies, when the plum tree finally blossoms but every last plum is eaten by squirrels, when you find that the weeds you pulled were the lace flowers you planted last spring, you wonder if your effort matters at all. When the acorns you buried with your son rot in the ground, when you kill a houseplant with too much loving care, when you discover that oak trees are meant to live in forests and not front yards, you worry you may be doing more harm than good. Are we God's helpers in the garden, like Adam, like Eve? Or are we the reason why, as St. Paul writes, all of creation groans?[2]

If peace is a state of harmony, if it is a kind of wholeness or completeness, then peaceful places are spacious places where our whole selves can abide.

At Maplehurst, peace sings its promises in the treetops, but those treetops are far above my head. Meanwhile, I am down below, often stumbling over roots, frequently making mistakes, and not at all sure whether the seeds I am sowing from moment to moment will ever take root and grow. But my heart is still tuned to the distant song, and I have begun to suspect that the trees themselves have a great deal to tell me. I hope that by listening to them as I articulate this story, I can discover some new harmony exactly right for the making of this place Jonathan and I call home.

Chapter 1

Citrus Grove

RECEIVING THE GIFT
OF LIMITS

Maplehurst, the farmhouse I call home, was built circa 1880 by a Pennsylvania Quaker named Mark Hughes. "Circa" is a handy term, a concise way of saying that Maplehurst was certainly built before 1882, when it first shows up in official records, but may have been built as early as 1878. A local map from just prior to that year marks out the land as belonging to the Hughes family but does not show the house Mark Hughes built for his wife, Priscilla, and their two daughters. One more daughter would be born to them while they were living within these red brick walls.

Compared with typical Victorian home design, this house has a Quaker plainness. There are no decorative plasterwork ceilings, no intricate gingerbread trimmings, no carved mahogany mantelpieces. And yet there are extravagant touches, such as the curved top of every window frame, the spaciousness of the front hall, and the impressive length of the driveway. These details suggest that Mark and Priscilla Hughes were not Quakers in quite the same mold as their forebears. Members of the local Friends meeting house built many other red brick houses in this town, but their windows are framed by simple rectangles and they sit without pretension quite close to the main road.

Mark Hughes did not cause the sun to rise in the east or set in the west, but he placed his home precisely so that the light of the sun and the moon would flood the elegant curve of his windows. Farmer Hughes did not mound the soil into the hill or "hurst" that gave this house its name, but he paced the rise and marked it out for his foundation. The view of green fields rolling down in every direction must have pleased him as it pleases me, though the fields today are dotted with new houses rather than Guernsey cattle. In all these ways, Mark and Priscilla Hughes were placemakers. They shaped this place, and their careful choices created a home that has since sheltered many families, most recently my own.

I do not know if their nineteenth-century religion gave the Hughes family a spiritual vocabulary for the care they took in making this place. Did they understand their placemaking choices as expressions of love and faith? Or did Priscilla feel a mite guilty about those elegant windows? Did Mark worry about the costs of red bricks and slate tiles? Might the simple wooden slab used for a fireplace mantel in the parlor be their nod to thrift and practicality, a compensation for other indulgences? I don't know. But I do know that Pennsylvania Quakers were committed to peace, and peaceful is the first word I would choose to describe this green hilltop and the quiet farms and meandering roads of the surrounding towns and villages.

The spiritual vocabulary I gleaned from the church of my

childhood did not have many words to describe the care and keeping of places or the people who find shelter in them. There was the spiritual practice of hospitality, but that was a word that made me nervous. I did not then know to call myself an introvert. I understood only that I was shy, and that this trait was a serious liability for Christian service. Home was always my favorite place to be, but I saw no connection between my love for home and my love for God. Instead, I understood that it was through preaching, teaching, and foreign travel that one loved and served God best. My own father did these things, but caring for the house and tending the garden were his favorite pastimes. He chose the wallpaper for our front hall, pruned roses in the flowerbeds, and made a dollhouse and backyard playhouse for his three daughters. But these were not the qualities that marked him as a devout and faithful man. Or so I thought when I was a child.

My father was born in the last months of the Second World War and grew up the middle child of five on a farm in the dusty prairie of north central Texas. His father grew cash crops such as cotton, peanuts, and watermelon, but as on many small family farms in those days, he and my grandmother also planted peach trees, kept a milk cow, and grew their own vegetables. My father has only rarely spoken of picking cotton, barehanded, with his siblings, but he tells me again and again about his grandmother, my great-grandmother, who surrounded her Comanche County farmhouse with scented petunias, fragrant geraniums, and one particular blue iris that was so strongly perfumed, my father says, "It would just about knock a little boy right over." By the time I was a girl playing hide-and-seek among the hay bales with my cousins, my grandfather was long dead. I don't remember ever seeing cotton in the field, but I do remember my father planting blue morning glories that grew up and over my grandmother's chain-link fence.

When my father visits us here at Maplehurst, he almost always plants something, usually a tree. On his first visit, it was a peach. On his second, it was a fig. The variety is called Chicago Hardy, and the name always causes me to hope for more figs than the tree seems capable of bearing. So I downsize my desire and accept that one fig is all I need to taste the honey-sweet memories of the fig tree that grew in the Texas backyard of my childhood. That's where my father first taught me, without words, that creation is good, and that I was made to enjoy it and participate in it. Like most spiritual truths received in youth, it was one I would forget and need to relearn many times over the years.

Since moving to our old farmhouse, I often recall the poet T. S. Eliot's message from *Four Quartets*: we will spend our lives exploring only to find, at the end, we have returned to our beginning, but this time with understanding. I have traveled so far from the pecan trees of my childhood, yet I understand the significance of my own origins in new and deeper ways every time I plant a tree at Maplehurst. At eighteen, I would have been horrified to learn that one day I would want little more than to sit on a farmhouse porch and watch morning glories crest and curl over a fence. That was the age I moved from the room overlooking my father's garden to a cinderblock dorm room in College Station, Texas. I shared the room with April, my best friend from high school, and two other girls who had been temporarily assigned to our double room because of overcrowding in the university's dormitory system. April and I had spent the previous summer collecting odd posters and other paper ephemera that would, we were quite sure, give our shared room a quirky and welcoming vibe. Alas, our grand ambition to create a gathering place did not survive those first few weeks of sardine-can living.

Jonathan and I married with three semesters of college left to finish. The nearest we came then to an appreciation of the natural world was the wood-grain Con-Tact paper we used to cover the glow of the orange laminate countertops in our first apartment kitchen. When we had toured the apartment months before our wedding, the manager told us that every apartment would soon be remodeled. I don't think I asked or even cared what our remodeled kitchen would look like. All that mattered to me was that it would be new. In those days, before I had lived in a home of my own or made a single decorating decision (beyond the cabbage rose wallpaper in my childhood bedroom), new was the one and only thing I valued in a home. When we registered for wedding gifts at a local department store, the registration forms asked about the colors in our home. *What colors decorate your kitchen? What colors adorn your master bedroom?* I suppose that information was meant to help those gift-buyers who desired to go "off-list." I left the questions blank. The only thing I felt sure of was that new things had the best chance of pleasing me. New things would prove this home belonged to me—and not to my parents or the university or some other authority. New things for our new life together.

It was late the night we came home from our honeymoon and entered that College Station apartment for the first time as husband and wife. I remember only the delight of finding that my mother had surreptitiously accessed the apartment and neatly made our four-poster bed with sheets and blankets from our gift registry. It wasn't until the bright light of the next morning that I noticed the kitchen countertops had not been replaced. The intensity of my disappointment was hardly tempered by the fact that we would only live in this place for the fifteen weeks of a single academic semester. In May, we would move to the East

Texas town of Orange for the three months of my husband's engineering internship. In August, we would return to College Station and to some new apartment for our final two semesters. When I look back, I do not see my disappointment as a regrettable lack of contentment. Instead, I see a young couple who had no idea that the God they had begun to follow together would, again and again, use beauty to save them and the pursuit of beauty to guide them. I see a young woman who, with hesitation, admitted she did not like her orange countertops. And I see a young man who understood and said, "I have an idea."

I have lately had my eye on a little-known tree called *Franklinia alatamaha*, offered for sale in the Monrovia plant catalog. Before the catalog arrived in my mailbox at Maplehurst, I had heard the tree's story and seen several growing in a small grove at a local arboretum. One of my favorite books (alas, it is too enormous for my bedside table) is *Dirr's Encyclopedia of Trees and Shrubs.* Michael Dirr informs me that the *Franklinia* tree is "handsome" but "persnickety," and so, doubting my skills as a gardener and the merits of my sticky clay soil, I have hesitated to purchase my own. *Franklinia* is a small tree with open, airy branches. In fall, the leaves turn from green to bright red or orange. Best of all, in late summer it carries exquisite white flowers with brilliant yellow stamens. They look to me a bit like the flowers of a single flat Japanese peony.

The story of this tree is tied to the story of another Pennsylvania Quaker family, specifically, a father and son named John and William Bartram. I first heard the name Bartram while Jonathan and I were living in northeastern Florida. Our neighborhood was quite close to a scenic highway named for the son, William. William is credited with being the United States' first native-born naturalist, a career he embarked on when his Florida orange-growing estate failed to thrive. Bright new beginnings are often disguised as defeats, aren't they?

In 1765, most of what now comprises the state of Florida was a British colony newly acquired from Spain. John Bartram was appointed "Royal Botanist" by King George III of Great Britain and given a stipend to travel the territory and report his findings. Together, John and William explored and documented the flora and fauna of the southeast, from Florida to Philadelphia. While traveling the Alatamaha River (now called Altamaha) in Georgia that same year, the Bartrams discovered a small, delightful tree with cup-shaped white flowers. A few years later, William returned to collect seeds, which he brought back with him and promptly planted in his father's Philadelphia garden. Having never seen a tree like this one, the Bartrams named it for an extraordinary American character and John's friend, Benjamin Franklin. The seeds took root, and the *Franklinia* tree thrived in its new urban soil. However, in 1803, when other tree lovers returned to Georgia to collect more seeds, the original *Franklinias* had mysteriously disappeared. The tree was extinct in the wild, and every *Franklinia* growing today is descended from the seeds planted in John Bartram's Philadelphia garden.

I take a possessive sort of pleasure in the history of the *Franklinia* because, like the Bartrams, it wasn't long ago that I traveled the same route from northeastern Florida—where we lived in a house stuccoed in pale pink seashells near the site of William's failed citrus farm—to Maplehurst in Pennsylvania, quite close to John's Philadelphia garden, which is open to visitors. The Bartrams remind me that home is as much temporal as geographical. We live in particular places, but we also live in particular times, and I cannot imagine living among the Spanish moss-covered oaks of northern Florida without the comforts my time provides, comforts like central air conditioning, sunscreen, and bug spray. I only lived in Florida for two years, yet I felt at the time as if loneliness and winter allergies might kill me. Surely mosquitos, or alligators, or heat would have done so in a former time.

Though we live in very different historical moments, I do recognize something familiar in John and William Bartram: when beauty beckoned, they paused and paid attention. On a botanical mission that was likely focused on discovering new sources for food and medicine, they saw a beautiful tree in flower and never forgot the sight of it. Our world today would be ever so slightly impoverished if William had not pursued those seeds, gathered them up, and planted them at his father's home.

> *This magnetic pull toward beauty is an inclination most of us carry but too few of us acknowledge. Even if we are aware of it, we seldom honor it as something planted in us for a purpose.*

This magnetic pull toward beauty is an inclination most of us carry but too few of us acknowledge. Even if we are aware of it, we seldom honor it as something planted in us for a purpose. The rushing world has convinced us that beauty is something extra, not the thing itself. I would never have guessed, and perhaps the Bartrams did not even guess, that the hand that compels us to stop and stare at something as insignificant as a beautiful tree in flower, might be the hand of God. Rarely do we know what is at stake when beauty surprises us into stillness and we pause to listen, even for a moment, to creation's song.

When I recall the first few years of our marriage, I sometimes see only a string of insignificant and anonymous apartments. But I have come to understand that no place on earth is insignificant, and no shelter is truly anonymous. Beauty can be found almost anywhere. During the three months we lived in Orange, Texas, having said goodbye to our first apartment by peeling away the Con-Tact paper from those orange countertops, I was acutely aware of all that was wrong with our second apartment home. But today I remember the small ways in which we made it wonderful, one of which I discovered only inadvertently through the embarrassing tale of a small child.

There was a little girl I sometimes babysat in our apartment during that summer. She was the daughter of Jonathan's coworker at the chemical plant where he was a research assistant in polymer science. Polymer, as this little girl well knew, is a scientist's word for plastics. Strangely, but appropriately, our apartment was itself made almost entirely of plastic. The kitchen cabinets looked like beautifully carved oak, but they were plastic. The open shelves dividing kitchen from living room were plastic. The doorknobs were plastic. The towel rack in the bathroom was plastic. The apartment's tiny patio was planted with plastic grass in a too-cheerful shade of green.

Jonathan came home from work one day with a mystifying story. His coworker, the father of this little girl, had, with much gleeful winking, told everyone in the company lunch room that Jonathan and his wife had a bed that hung from the ceiling. The coworkers laughed at the story, and Jonathan could not imagine where the rumor had come from, but when he shared it with me, I immediately saw my bedroom from another, much more delightful angle—that of a four-year-old girl. Had Jonathan and I also been three feet tall, we no doubt would have realized sooner that our four-poster bed with its white canopy did not in fact rest solidly on the (plastic) carpeted floor. No, as this little girl had observed, we had a summer swing that hung from the ceiling. We had a soft nest in the trees. We had a fluffy cloud gently drifting beneath a popcorn ceiling. Once I heard the story, I no longer felt guilty for using a precious wedding gift certificate to buy that gauzy white canopy rather than some practical gadget. Guests are a gift, even if they are children, because they allow us to see our home through new eyes.

Three hours of highway lay between our first apartment in College Station and our second in Orange. If we had driven our green pickup truck on that highway even fifteen minutes longer, we would have found ourselves in Louisiana, towing a rental trailer with little more than our four-poster bed and the wedding china every southern bride received in those days. On the day of our move, we drove straight to Orange without stopping, eager to settle into the apartment we had rented by phone but never seen. Unfortunately, we failed to consider the apartment manager's office hours. He had left for the day thirty minutes before our arrival. We had no key and no money for a motel room, but Jonathan thought he remembered our apartment number. Sure enough, our search for that number led us to a first-floor apartment that seemed to be empty, at least as far as we could tell by peering through the slatted blinds that hung on the other side of a sliding glass door. When we discovered that the glass door was unlocked, we carried our mattress and our boxes across the threshold, fingers crossed that this was indeed our home.

During those three months in Orange, we were confronted by some of the ways in which humans *unmake* a place. There was the choking stench that drifted from the smokestacks of local industry. There were shards of plastic amongst the sea glass and seashells littering the nearest beach. There was the clear but unmarked boundary between the houses for white people and the houses for black and brown people. Racism hung in the air as palpably as the noxious factory fumes. A few days after Jonathan began his internship at the chemical plant, a coworker asked him where we did our grocery shopping. When Jonathan told him, the man said, "Oh, no. You don't want to shop there. That's for the Mexicans." Stunned, Jonathan didn't say a word. He did not say, "Ah, well, you see, my mother was born in Mexico, so perhaps that store is exactly where I *do* want to shop." We went to church with the white folks, but our welcome turned ever so slightly sour when the pastor found out my husband had been baptized in another denomination. *Perhaps he would want to consider being baptized again?* But we had only three months in this place, and rebaptism was not on our list of priorities.

Perhaps it was the abbreviated nature of our stay that compelled us into placemaking, to repeat the task we had just completed—to find beauty in making a home together and then share it with other people. Only a couple of young innocents could imagine such a thing was possible in so narrow a slice of time. When we joined the Wednesday night gathering for college students at our new church, we sat uncomfortably on metal folding chairs in a nearly empty beige room for only fifteen minutes before suggesting that the whole group—all four of us—might prefer to gather instead in our plastic apartment. The church authorities surprised us by refusing our offer, but we dodged their concerns by posting a note on the door of the now thoroughly empty beige room: *For the summer, the college group is meeting at the Purifoys' home. Please join us! Citrus Grove Apartments, Unit 103.*

Sacred spaces need not be perfect, but they cease to be sacred if no one cares for them. That beige church room may have been serviceable, but it was far from sacred. Our apartment may have been plastic, but Jonathan and I made it sacred by doing our best to care for it. That summer, we even bought a vacuum cleaner capable of handling polyester shag. I no longer recall how quickly we grew from a gathering of four to a crowd of twenty-four, but it must have been lightning quick. I don't think I had even unpacked the wedding china by the time we pushed our tiny two-seater sofa back against the wall to make room for more people to sit on the floor. There were locals who attended college elsewhere but were living at home with their parents for the summer. There were several recent high school graduates who planned to join the same university Jonathan and I attended in the fall. There were a few other interns like Jonathan who were also working at the chemical plant. And there were a couple of teenagers who had never visited the church but couldn't seem to stay away from our group.

Sacred spaces need not be perfect, but they cease to be sacred if no one cares for them.

I remember no names, only a handful of faces and a few stories: the engineer and the intern who fell in love and would later marry, the young man who set aside college to fix his dreams on making music, another young man who began carrying baked goods or bags of groceries to neighborhoods on the other side of that unmarked, yet all-too-real, color line. We sometimes helped him by knocking on doors, introducing ourselves, and asking, "Would you care for some fresh fruit?" We were awkward and inexperienced, but we had tapped into a source of abundant life that was not only bigger than we were but also deeply rooted within this place. It felt as if some underground river had long been waiting for this very moment to break forth and surge ahead. Were we instigators? Were we remaking this place? I'm not sure. But I know we were witnesses as new life bubbled up and overflowed. Ever since, it has been easier for me to believe in the inherent worth and significance of the humblest place a person might call home.

Even the most powerful rivers have limits. In Orange, our primary limit was time—just three months. Marriage, too, is a limitation of sorts. In faith, we bind our hearts and hands together and curtail our independence in the hope that something new and fruitful will emerge. Maplehurst as well, the destination of all these years Jonathan and I have traveled together, is a place restrained as surely as any river by its banks. Restrained by a split-rail fence we have no money or time to repair. Restrained by odors from neighboring mushroom farms drifting in over the heads of our dinner guests. Restrained by beautiful old wood that is far too liable to rot. But I have come to recognize that life without limits is formless. Without limits, our purpose in each place we plant our feet is more difficult to discern. Our life's current, and those good works God prepared in advance for us to do, are much harder to find. When we pray for guidance, perhaps God's answer is every way he hems us in, like a river.

Who am I to say if even thirty years at Maplehurst will bear as much good fruit as the three months we spent in Orange, Texas? How can I know what ephemeral flowers bloomed in Orange before our time there or what flowers appeared after? All I know is I was given a glimpse of something beautiful, and I gathered the seeds. I will plant those seeds at Maplehurst, and they will always remind me that limits are a gift. Limits lead us to the water. Like a tree, I will send out my roots toward the stream, grateful for every hard rock and difficult stone that tells me *this is the way, walk in it.*[1]

Chapter 2

Pine Tree

CHOOSING TO WANT

This morning, I stumbled over a dead rhododendron in the backyard. It was spectacularly dead. There was no need to look closely. No reason to snap a branch and look for that living wick of green in its middle. For some reason, I have always associated the name rhododendron with the age of dinosaurs, and this one was as dusty brown and shriveled as an ancient museum specimen. When I planted the little thing, it was covered in pale, lemony blossoms, but knowing that rhododendrons have very particular tastes in sunlight and soil, I guarded my heart against loving it. I told Jonathan, "This is an experiment. It will probably fail." Yet I secretly dreamed of watching flowers like spring sunshine dance in the shadows beneath the dense evergreen needles of a pair of Norway spruce. Jonathan's smile was confident and admiring, and I gave thanks that I had not married a gardener. A hard worker, yes. But not a gardener. I did not tell him what I suspect he had never noticed: this was not the only rhododendron

I had attempted in our yard. If this new plant died, it would not be the first.

Now that the little yellow rhododendron is finished, I'm afraid my vision for this dark corner of the yard has also withered. I could try the white softball flowers of Annabelle hydrangeas, but now I worry that the soil down here is too compacted and dried out by tree roots to grow anything but wispy weeds. Dead plants are a fact of gardening life, but lately my sense of failure has only grown, like a spreading stain. The rhododendron was a mistake. Somehow, admitting that to myself draws me nearer to another admission. One I do not want to make. One I can hardly bear to consider. When I stand over the rhododendron, the house is at my back. And here is the true nexus of my grief (though I must turn away from the warm red bricks before I can bring myself to think it): *This house may be the real mistake.*

Maplehurst is falling apart, and we do not know what to do. An agent from our insurance company came by last week for his biannual inspection. Apparently, this is something insurance companies do with older homes. Insurers know a truth about old houses that Jonathan and I are only beginning to grasp: look away for an instant, and they age twenty years. Limestone mortar crumbles. Handmade bricks crack. Porches rot. Yesterday, the agent's report arrived by mail. It was sternly worded: "If homeowners fail to maintain their woodwork, rot and decay can set in immediately. You have one year to make repairs, or your policy may be terminated."

We love this old house, and we are failing it.

I was deceived by the trees. Or perhaps they are not to blame. Maybe I misunderstood. When we first visited Maplehurst looking for an old farmhouse to call home, twenty-eight maple trees in fourteen pairs streamed alongside the driveway like living symbols of permanence and solidity. They looked as if they had stood guard over this house forever and always would. That illusion did not last long. We moved in just in time to watch the silver maples shift to golden yellow. Before we had even unpacked all of our boxes, the trees had dropped every distinctive, two-tone leaf (first green then gold on top and silver beneath). All winter, I looked on those bare limbs as promises waiting to be kept, but when spring storms blew through, we lost three trees in quick succession. Our beautiful, enormous maples were hollowed out by age. The trees, like any other mortal creature, would not live forever, and we had arrived just in time to watch them die.

The trees were teaching us the cost of caring for a place, and the lessons therein were so very hard to learn. Not only was there expensive and time-consuming cleanup every time a tree or large limb fell, there was a high price to pay for the professional pruning that could extend the life of these trees. Meanwhile, behind the leafy shadows, water was dripping, drop by drop, on the beams supporting our roof. The century-old copper lining the box gutters finally, silently, cracked right through. One morning, a hefty chunk of the tall wooden molding lining the eaves of our roof fell and shattered at my feet. The gap left behind was like the jagged, black space where a bright white tooth should be.

Who wants to labor over complicated repairs when grass is begging you to dig it up and plant roses? Overwhelmed and unsure, I chose to set aside the needs of the house. I wanted to create pleasant new places, and these new places were fairly easy to make. I hung a hammock, I chose a spot for a new flowerbed, and we decided on just the right corner for an Amish-made chicken coop. I did not want to care for old things or dying things because that kind of wanting was risky. Disappointment and frustration seemed likely, if not inevitable. I noticed the peeling paint, I registered the cracked windowpanes, and I cringed when I glanced up and saw the louvered shutter dangling at a crazy angle from our bedroom window. But I did not know what to do, and so I looked away.

The home we moved into after our return to college from Orange, Texas, wasn't the fulfillment of a dream or the satisfaction of desire. We were only biding our time until graduation, and very little was at stake. This is one of the gifts of humble beginnings—your heart is, at least temporarily, quite safe. Our third apartment was a practical white box near enough to campus for my husband to ride his bike and far enough from campus for the rent to be affordable. And so we settled into our new home in the Pine Tree Apartments.

Were there pine trees? I've searched my memories, but I can't recall. In those honeymoon days, I don't think I paid much attention to the natural world beyond my own four walls. I only dimly registered the fact that our three-month-old kitchen table—which had not survived our move back from Orange—had been made of pine and particle board, while the old pedestal table we brought home from a local secondhand shop to replace it was made of sturdy, solid oak. Young and newly married, we were focused on the future, yet we were still troubled by the black scuff marks our meager furnishings had left on the apartment's white walls after moving day. At some point during the first few weeks in our new home, Jonathan walked over to the apartment manager's office (Did he shuffle dry pine needles as he walked?

Perhaps he did.) and asked, politely, "Would it be possible for me to get a can of white paint?"

"Why?" the manager asked, expressing only surprise.

"Because our walls have a few scuff marks, and I'd like to cover them up," my husband said.

At the time, and even in retrospect, our request for a can of paint seems like such a small and ordinary thing. But the response was an extraordinary grace. The manager handed over a can of paint with a smile, and then made us an offer we had never anticipated and certainly wouldn't refuse. *Would we be willing to let him show our apartment to prospective tenants?* In exchange, he would give us a substantial discount on our rent. For two full-time students, the offer was as appreciated as it was unexpected. If our story had ended there, I might be tempted to declare that caring for one's home always makes good financial sense. Certainly it did for us that year. But since then I have discovered, again and again, that choosing to care for a place often makes no financial sense at all. Instead, it will cost you. It will cost you money. It will cost you time. It will bring you pleasure, but it might also bring you grief. If keeping a home and a place well makes sense, it is only in the way that love makes sense. When we love someone, we serve them, we care for them, and, on our better days at least, we do not count the cost.

If keeping a home and a place well makes sense, it is only in the way that love makes sense. When we love someone, we serve them, we care for them, and, on our better days at least, we do not count the cost.

Recently, at Maplehurst, all I've done is count the cost.

When I write of the maple trees that give this home its name, perhaps you picture the dark autumn leaves of the red maple growing in your front yard or the sunshine-yellow spring flowers of the Norway maple planted at a local park. This might give you a good sense of the trees I am writing about, or it might not. It all depends on where you live. With his usual sly wit, Michael Dirr, in his *Encyclopedia of Trees and Shrubs*, tells me, "A red maple from Florida is not the same as a red maple from Maine . . . A red maple from Florida will die in Maine, and vice versa."[1] There aren't only the differences within a species to consider. There are also the distinctive qualities of the place where it will grow. Do you live on land that longs for the comforting weight of a forest? Do you live on land that dreams of prairie grass blowing in a high wind? Perhaps you live where the rocky soil wants only the caress of mountain wildflowers. You can stick the same maple seedling in any of these places, and, perhaps with a little assistance, a maple tree will grow. But how tall will it grow and how quickly? How expansive will its canopy be? What birds, what insects, will make a home in its branches? Our desires shape the land, but the desires of the land itself are powerful too.

I'd never really thought about the relationship between particular places and their particular trees until a recent visit to see my parents in the Midwest. My mother and father no longer live in Texas. They relocated more than a decade ago to a house in a leafy suburb of Kansas City, Kansas. I say "leafy" intentionally because, if you're like me, the name *Kansas* calls to mind only images of flat land and waving grass. But this is not an accurate picture of eastern Kansas near the Missouri state line. My parents' house is nestled among green hills and rocky outcroppings. The little creek that trickles through their backyard is overhung with maples of all sorts. I was there during an especially rainy spring. The green hills reminded me so much of the Pennsylvania foothills I call home—and yet they didn't. I wondered why the elements of the landscape looked familiar and yet somehow did not add up to a whole that I would ever confuse with Pennsylvania. Here were hills. They were green. The mixture of deciduous and evergreen trees seemed about the same, at least in and around the city and suburbs. Yet, if I had been set down in any spot, I would have been sure I was in the Midwest. Why?

The answer came to me as my parents drove me back to the airport. A vague question floated through my mind: *Where are all the old trees?* And then I realized the difference that had eluded me. Not all the trees we drove past were young, they couldn't be, but all the trees we passed were shorter than many of the trees that grow near my Pennsylvania home. Without realizing it, I had been assuming all week that the trees I saw were juveniles. The answer, I realized then, was *rain*. Kansas, even in its greener, eastern side, does not receive as much rainfall as the mid-Atlantic piedmont, our hilly, sloping region between the mountains and the sea. That means the oldest, tallest trees near my Pennsylvania home will always be taller than the oldest and tallest trees near my parents' home. When I lived in Texas and Illinois, the landscapes were similar to the Kansas landscape: it was the sky that was large. Here, amid these Pennsylvania hills, the sky opens up only when you drive along a ridge or crest a high hill. The proportions of this land are quaint and cozy, but step into a forest or drive through a patch of old trees, and those quaint proportions vanish. In this place where frequent showers draw trees up to enormous heights, the air beneath the cathedral canopy of the trees feels more spacious than a sky that only ever reveals itself in glimpses.

Our dreams and desires for a place are likely to be inappropriate, perhaps even destructive, if we haven't first looked for evidence of what the land itself wants. Placemakers must first see. They must look past the ubiquitous chain store toward the shape of the hills beyond. They must register the music of raindrops on hard clay soil even if they feel the sting of rain delays or canceled plans. Placemakers must see a place as it is, taking in all that already makes a place special, not only what might be possible. Visitors and newcomers often have this way of seeing. The English rector of our Pennsylvania church has not lived long in North America, but he recently told me a curious fact: London may be known for its rain, but where we live, in eastern Pennsylvania, our occasional rain showers add up to more inches than London's constant drizzle. I'm not sure what London land, buried deep by centuries of habitation, dreams of. Perhaps it is so deeply buried it sleeps a dreamless sleep. But my rector and I live on land that still yearns for the forests that sheltered indigenous tribes and greeted European colonists. On the edges of the cornfields and the convenience stores and the culs-de-sac where kids circle on tricycles, you can see what the land still desires to be. And those edges are vigorous. When I weed my flowerbeds, I'm as likely to pull out seedling maples and oaks and tulip poplars as I am dandelions.

Placemakers must see a place as it is, taking in all that already makes a place special, not only what might be possible.

The baby oak trees, carried by squirrels perhaps, are especially difficult to eradicate. A seedling might have only two distinctive oak leaves, but it will already have a long taproot, like a skinny carrot, wedged anchor-deep into the ground. I've never pulled one out without recognizing the enormousness of lost potential. Of course, I can't let an oak tree even begin to spread its roots directly beneath my roof overhang or in a crack between the flagstones that lead to our front door. But though the taproots seem so vital, I've never found success replanting them. Still, I can never toss them on my compost pile with a completely clear conscience. I always remember the perspective of one of my favorite garden writers, Henry Mitchell. For decades, Mitchell was the gardening columnist for *The Washington Post*, and he is well remembered for his tongue-in-cheek diatribes against trees. According to Mitchell, trees were well and good in forests or city parks, but enormous maples and towering oaks had no business in an ordinary backyard. He preferred open, airy sunlight for his much-loved irises. In one memorable piece, he cautioned against ever planting an oak tree, even if you did have space enough for a large tree plus your irises. The oak tree, he said, is a majestic thing, but in 300 years or so when it dies, it will break some gardener's heart.

Abundant rain and abundant light have made all the trees around this old farmhouse extraordinary. The hemlocks, the pines, the spruces, the maples, the cherries, even our marvelous, twisted old pear tree. Together they shelter this place like the gilded vault of a medieval church. But there is one tree that exceeds them all. It grows about a hundred yards from our back fence, just beyond the neighborhood street that circles our property, and on the edge of the public golf course around which all these new homes have been built. This tree does not belong to Maplehurst, though it grows in dirt that once belonged to Mark Hughes and his famous Guernsey cattle. It is a white oak, and its many limbs are curled like a wind-tossed head of hair. The leaves seem to me to be a mossy gray-green, though perhaps I have only imagined the gray because I know what it says on a plaque at the base of this tree: *White Oak Planted Year 1643.*

Naturalist Donald Peattie once wrote, "If oak is the king of trees, as tradition has it, then the eastern white oak . . . is the king of kings."[2] Perhaps that explains why the golf course, though it carves its way through stands of many different trees, has chosen to use the silhouette of a spreading white oak tree within its logo. Not only is our golf course tree a king of kings, it is also a renowned "Penn Oak," and one of the few remaining trees that was already reaching green leaves toward blue sky when William Penn last visited his fledgling New World colony. Some days, I imagine that the image of this particular tree is the symbol of everything I hold dear, a somewhat grandiose vision Peattie, nevertheless, seems to affirm. "Indeed," he writes, "the fortunate possessor of an old white oak owns a sort of second home, an outdoor mansion of shade and greenery and leafy music."[3] But every year, a few more of this particular mansion's gnarled branches are bare of leaves. Golfers in bright polo shirts come and go, swinging their clubs beneath these leaves while I only wait. *How long will it be before this tree breaks my heart?*

Many of us long to put down roots in some particular place, but we guard ourselves against heartbreak by waiting for a perfect place. The imperfections of a place will hurt us so much more if we have freed our hearts and sunk ourselves deep. Perhaps it's my doubts about this home of ours that have reminded me of our Pine Tree Apartments days. Back then, we had many dreams and desires, but none of them were rooted in the place where we lived. Ours were not farmhouse dreams. Ours weren't dreams of home at all, or at least I didn't think so at the time. When we first married, we dreamed of travel. Big cities. Faraway countries. I was studying for a degree in British literature and history, and so we talked especially of England, Scotland, and Ireland. *Could we live there someday? Maybe work there or go to school there?* Our dreams were not neat and ordered. One moment we wanted to live in a city high-rise and exchange our truck for the subway, and the next we wanted to wander misty, emerald hills. Essentially, we wanted new, different, and extraordinary—anything but the familiar Texas prairie that had sheltered us for so long.

Many of us long to put down roots in some particular place, but we guard ourselves against heartbreak by waiting for a perfect place.

Back then, if you had asked me about Texas, I would have enumerated only its flaws: the country was too hot and the cities too sprawling; the summers were too long and the winters too brown. If pressed, I might also have praised bluebonnets in spring and live oak trees that dipped and twisted and grew any way but straight. But only if pressed. Familiarity sometimes breeds indifference, a kind of blindness (*Were there pine trees?*). Familiarity can also breed disdain. One of the small, good things about certain losses is that they give us eyes to see. Texas is no longer mine. I have now lived away from it for more years than I lived in it, and it is no longer where my parents or most of my siblings live. My youngest sibling, my only brother, still lives and works among the oil refineries of south Texas, but when I talk to him, I sense how tenuous his hold on the place has become. His voice is Texan through and through, as if thickened by years of heat and humidity, but he talks about buying a little Kansas land. He wouldn't mind an annual taste of winter.

If you asked me now, I would tell you how the clear, cold rivers of the Texas Hill Country carve their way through limestone.

I would tell you that a grove of live oaks looks more like a field of grazing animals than a forest of trees. I would tell you about the flaky Czech pastry called *kolache*, and what it's like when a thousand bats rise in a swift-moving cloud from beneath a city bridge at twilight. I would tell you these things because I've learned something in the intervening years: every place made by God is loved by God, and that includes every place where his people dwell. If we are willing to look through the lens of his love, then we will see that every place has some particular magic.

Every place made by God is loved by God, and that includes every place where his people dwell. If we are willing to look through the lens of his love, then we will see that every place has some particular magic.

But what happens when a place is broken in ways a can of paint alone could never fix? Perhaps a mustard seed of peace is planted when we see something wrong—small as a scuff mark or large as deforestation or famine—and we do not wallow in either despair or bitterness but instead ask for help, ask for paint, try our own unskilled hands at repair and restoration. Once I was blind. Blind to the difficult beauty unique to my home state; blind even to the tranquil beauty of an orange laminate countertop, well-scrubbed and set with a jar of grocery store flowers in a wedding gift vase. But I was not fully blind, and that has made all the difference. I could at least see a little of what was wrong and what was ugly, and I had married someone who was not too timid to ask for paint, even though he had never held a paintbrush.

That first success at the Pine Tree Apartments emboldened us. How many rooms have we painted since? After the white walls of Pine Tree came my hunt for the perfect shade of beige in Virginia. I learned to choose a boring beige over a pretty one, because the pretty one will almost always look pink or purple on the wall. Later there was a tiny Chicago apartment painted gray-blue and gray-green. In a larger Chicago apartment, I painted our dining room rose. Later, feeling those expansive walls close in on me, I covered the rose in robin's egg blue. In Florida, I discovered that my new home would be for me a wilderness rather than a paradise, but my misery was soothed by the most delicate, watery shade of aqua. And at Maplehurst, my dining room is a deep, inky color that is sometimes black, sometimes blue, and sometimes charcoal gray. So many walls and so many cans of paint. I don't need to add up the average price of a can of Benjamin Moore to tell you that we have not received a financial return on this particular investment. But if we've lost money and time, what have we gained? I'm not sure, but I know that so many of my memories are tinted like a paint chip: I found the loveliest shade of green for the room that would belong to our first baby, but the room stayed empty for so long it nearly crushed me. Years later I gave birth to a son, our third child, in our own four-poster bed. The walls of that room were glad like dewdrops on yellow roses or golden bubbles of champagne.

One recent fall, it rained acorns. Tiny, delicate acorns in the smooth brown color that can only be called nutbrown, and large, golden acorns with rough caps tailor-made for the heads of gnomes or fairies. Everywhere I went, I gathered acorns. I couldn't help myself. I'd pick up one to study its silky shell, and three or four more would find their way into my pocket. I was so enchanted by the acorns I found—on walks through the neighborhood of homes around Maplehurst or on the sidewalks of my town as I headed toward the bakery or the secondhand bookstore—that I knew I wanted an oak tree for my own yard. Perhaps, somewhere deep within, I also wanted to steel my heart against the inevitable loss of the Penn Oak on the golf course. But what kind should I grow? The sheer variety of varieties is dizzying. The golf course oak is a white oak or *Quercus alba*. Did I want white oak or red? Pin oak or post oak? Each time I picked up a new acorn, I studied the tree above. Would I want that particular tree holding my grandchildren's swing?

I have always been overwhelmed by multiple options. I was the bride who tried on only three wedding dresses before she made her choice. Remembering this, I set down my tree books and did the only thing that made sense: I determined to let nature decide. Beau, the little boy who was born in that golden room, is always the one I call when I have seeds to plant. None of my children show much enthusiasm for my gardens, but Beau seems at least to accept gardening as necessary work. He is practical, literal-minded, and energetic. His attitude has always been, *Of course we plant seeds. We need to eat, don't we?* I filled Beau's hands with acorns in shades of honey and amber and caramel. He looked like a pirate with a horde of golden treasure. Together, we went looking for a place to bury them.

The spot we found was big enough for an oak but not very sunny. It was shaded by a tall horse chestnut tree, which one of my tree books says, "has a habit that makes [it] easy to identify."[4] I lived here for at least three years before I knew what to call it. Nearby, there was also a rather stunted pine tree and an enormous, spreading Norway maple, but with so many old trees on our property, full sun is hard to find. I decided this spot mimicked the conditions of the forest floor. Unless carried off by squirrels, acorns always drop in shade, and forests, though sun-loving, rear their young in the dim beneath their branches. And so we dug. Like squirrels, Beau and I buried our cache, but we also circled it with chicken wire. If one of those acorns sprouted, I didn't want the seedling to meet an early demise beneath the lawn mower. While Beau tilted the watering can and gave his mother a funny look, I said a prayer. I can't recall the words I spoke, but I think my prayer was both request and blessing. Somehow, it seemed like the appropriate thing to do. Nearly a year has passed since that day. The chicken wire remains, but nothing has grown. Not white oak, not red. Not post oak or pin. Not anything.

I know a lot about the odds of human reproduction. Even for healthy men and women, the odds don't favor babies. And I was not healthy for a long while. Even now, after so many years as a mother, I sometimes look at the crowd around my table with surprise. *How did this happen? How did so much waiting and wanting add up to such abundance?* These are the things I think about when I study the empty circle where a baby oak tree should be. Once I read a book about trees with a chapter on tree reproduction called "The Tree Lottery." Apparently, the odds of an acorn becoming a full-grown tree are close to the odds of winning the Powerball. Lotteries, at least, are drawn with regularity. Acorns, it turns out, are not. That fall must have been what is called a "mast" year for oaks in my area. Every two to five years, an oak tree produces a huge quantity of acorns but produces few acorns in between.[5] Each acorn is a wish for more, a dream of a tree, and a desire for an enduring legacy. Producing acorns requires a tremendous amount of energy and can leave a tree vulnerable to disease and harmful insects. Is the sacrifice worthwhile? These are the odds: according to German forester Peter Wohlleben, each tree in a forest rears exactly one adult tree to take its place. One forest beech might live 400 years, fruit sixty times, and produce 1.8 million beechnuts.[6] And at the end of its life, it will leave behind just one adult tree. The odds for poplars are even less favorable. A mother poplar might produce 54 million seeds annually and over a billion in its lifetime, and yet only one seed will ultimately bear mature fruit.[7] It doesn't sound at all worthwhile to me, and yet what other choice is there? The trees have no choice. Not really. But we do.

I resist the idea of living like a profligate tree, and I guard my heart against desire. I like to know that my labor is useful before I expend it. I never play the lottery. I tend to go for sure bets and guaranteed results. That's why I was so cautious when I planted the rhododendron. Once bitten, twice shy is my motto, and I may never again plant a shrub in that dark corner. Caring for Maplehurst and making it new has begun to seem like such a risky and perhaps even wasteful venture. We have two words for places like this: *money pit*. A money pit is a drain, a mistake, a fool's errand. It's a house in need of endless repairs. It's a garden that eats trees and shrubs and spits them back out like dinosaur bones. It reminds me of that proverb: "There are three things that are never satisfied, four that never say, 'Enough!': the grave, the barren womb, land, which is never satisfied with water, and fire, which never says, 'Enough!'"[8] I have been a woman with a barren womb. I prayed, I begged, and I was never satisfied by my emptiness. But after giving birth to three children, I gave up—not quite content but unwilling to struggle any longer with unmet desires. Now I look at my fourth child, my sweet second daughter, and I look at this majestic, if crumbling, old house, and I believe that both were God's idea, planted in me when I felt emptied of dreams, and it seemed so much safer to want nothing more.

Fruitfulness is sometimes the result of great effort and sometimes the gift of no effort at all. I might despair over buried acorns that will not grow, yet I keep on pulling up tap-rooted oaks from my flower beds. Scarcity and abundance are everywhere and all around us, and both have been a gift. Some of our Pine Tree Apartments dreams came true, and some did not. Some were fulfilled with ease, and others were realized only after a great and long-lasting struggle. We once made a home in a city high-rise, but we never did make a home overseas. Yet all these homes, as well as our many desires, have somehow come home with us to Maplehurst. Some part of them, some memory or knowledge or lesson learned, endures in this place where the green hills are as misty and emerald as any in Ireland. Jonathan and I no longer do as much traveling, nor do our conversations circle around places we might go. When we came to Maplehurst, we stood still while the world shifted and each new season made this place new. Here, I have known the particular drama and change only the rooted know, for I have watched trees grow and I have watched trees die. I am familiar with the first spring songs of the peeper frogs in the retention pond, and I can point to where the snow lasts longest before melting. I know this place. I love this place. I want more for this place.

I will choose to stay. I will plant my desires here, and I will not walk away. I will try to live like a forest tree. I will cast my seeds and cast my seeds and cast my seeds of love again. Like the land of the proverb, I will risk wanting more. I will refuse to cry "Enough!"

Chapter 3

Saucer Magnolia

LISTENING TO A PLACE

The poets tell us deciduous trees in autumn are flames or torches, and that "greenness is deeper than anyone knows."[1] The scientists tell us shorter days signal a tree to reclaim chlorophyll from its leaves, break it down into its constituent parts, and store those ingredients for use in the spring. In the scientific account, the color gold does not signify. It is merely waste to be discarded, down, down, onto some carefully raked pile that a small child will scatter with joy. But some scientists are not content with the superficial facts. With the poets, they desire to probe the depths of greenness. These scientists tell us that red and orange and gold *do* signify. They signify in the same way a burglar alarm signifies. According to this hypothesis, screaming colors are not waste—inconsequential pigment left behind—but pigment created for a purpose. Vivid autumn colors warn the aphids and their ilk: *Do not mess with this tree. In spring, it will flood your hiding place with toxins.*[2] I have needed the poets *and* the scientists in order to believe the evidence of my own eyes: October trees are bright flames, they are guiding lights, and they have also been, for me, a warning. Beauty signifies, and I have learned to look and listen well.

Our longing for more than the crispy, brown drifts of a Texas fall became a flaming torch, a proverbial pillar of fire, that led us forward. After graduation, Jonathan turned down the offer of a full-time position in the piney woods region of East Texas in favor of an engineering job in northern Virginia. The job was in the mountains, but we were drawn to the city, so we rented a small suburban townhouse halfway between the two. For the two years we lived there, we were halfway in every sense. Our bodies were halfway between city and country; our hearts were halfway between the two of us as a family and the extended families we had left behind. I was halfway between past and future, finishing up my final college classes by correspondence and researching graduate programs on the side. And though we didn't know it then, we were halfway between our old home on the Texas prairie and the Chicago neighborhood where we would feel fully at home for the first time in our lives. But if I'd had ears to hear it, I would have known that the beauty I was chasing was ringing an alarm. It was warning me that home is never simply a threshold you cross. It is a place you make and a place that might make—or unmake—you. In this halfway space, we would begin to learn the costs of stepping into the role God first gave in a garden: to be, like Adam and Eve, the makers and caretakers of a particular place. But we had not been given a paradise; instead, we had journeyed

> *Home is never simply a threshold you cross. It is a place you make and a place that might make—or unmake—you.*

into the most infamous halfway place of all, the place that is neither Egypt nor the Promised Land. We had chased our pillar of fire right into the wilderness.

We moved in June, and I immediately began counting down the days to fall. I had never, not once in my life, seen a tree burning in autumn colors. I had visited Washington D.C. only once before. When I was seventeen, I came to the city in late September for a student conference. One afternoon during that week, I was on an old yellow school bus returning with the other students from a service project on a coastal Maryland farm when I saw it: a flash of gold, more vivid even than the color of our bus. The road we were on shot through the woods like an arrow, but I could glimpse occasional bright flashes, as if a richly colored bird were flitting from tree to tree. I realized then that the green trees lining every road and city sidewalk would begin changing soon, but I would not witness it, having already flown home to Texas. I've never forgotten the ache that rose up in me, to be so near something I had always longed to see, and yet still miss it. Now, four years later, I had returned.

That first Virginia summer was summer like we had not known it could be. We may have moved to "the South," but we were farther north than we had ever lived before. On one of our first evenings in Virginia, Jonathan and I picked up dinner from a sandwich shop and drove toward the zigzag fences and grassy hills of a nearby national park, the site of two Civil War battles. It was a place that had been made by farmers, unmade by war, and remade by historians and naturalists. The peace we would always feel in that place was difficult to reconcile with its violent past.

We found a small gravel parking lot, walked to a picnic table on a hill, sat and ate and listened to the grass whisper its secrets to the breeze, and marveled that summer's warmth could feel so delightful. We had not known that cool air ever blew in summer.

"Let's build a patio," Jonathan said.

"What? But we're renting!"

"We could ask the landlord," he said. "There's space in the back-yard. Maybe if we offer to do the work, he'll pay for the supplies."

And that's what we did. Because if the breeze could blow in summer, then we needed a place where we could sit and catch it. What good is a summer breeze if you are inside eating dinner in front of your television set? Or seated at the table you've managed to squeeze into your windowless dining nook? It's as if the outside world is playing a game, and you've refused to play along.

First work, then play. We bought a small handsaw. Our landlord said to send him the receipts for wood, sand, and paving stones. We set to our task, clearing and preparing a small, square backyard that had grown into a wilderness of weeds and vines. For the first time in our lives, we sweated over a patch of dirt, but visions of a table and two chairs on a shady patio made the work sweet. Until a few days later. That is when I began to itch and scratch and eventually erupt with the terrible, seeping, angry-red trails of poison ivy. I knew about poison ivy only secondhand. My father had suffered terribly from the vines that grew in the woods behind our Texas home. When I was an adolescent, I had studied the oozing sores running down his arms and wondered why he did it. *Is clearing a spot in the woods for a chicken coop worth this kind of suffering? Why does he take the risk?* And risk it was. His allergic reactions were so terrible that he always needed a hefty round of steroids. Those steroid pills were infamous in our house because they could not be taken often without the risk of adverse side effects. We all knew that a clock began ticking the moment our father took the first pill. If poison ivy found him again at any point within the calendar year, he would not be able to take those same dangerous but wonderfully effective drugs.

Poison ivy is an American original. In 1784, William Bartram included it in a shipment of 220 valuable New World plants he had gathered to send back across the Atlantic to British plant collectors. In October of that year, when the rare hybrid Bartram oaks that still grow here must have begun dropping their strange combination of three different leaves, Bartram wrote a list to accompany his shipment. In flowing script, he recommends to European collectors first *"Rhus vernix,"* poison sumac, then five varieties of grape before including *"Rhus radicans,"* or poison ivy.[3] The proximity of grapes and poison ivy surprises me, but Bartram likely ordered his list in this way because both grow as vines, though we do not know whether he considered poison ivy a useful plant or merely a garden curiosity.

Like that other American native, the whitetail deer, poison ivy is far more prevalent today than it was when William Penn's colonists first arrived on these shores. Poison ivy thrives on the disturbed edges of cultivated land. It cannot endure the deep shade of a forest, nor can it survive in the middle of a field plowed for corn. Poison ivy is a native not only to the American wilderness but to the wilderness of halfway places that grow up around every new housing development and shopping center, highway and train track. Such wilderness is the shadow cast by our collective progress. Studies have shown that poison ivy is especially sensitive to the levels of carbon dioxide in our air. The higher the concentration, the more vigorous the plant, and the more virulent its poison. Since the 1960s, the poison in poison ivy has doubled its strength.[4]

If William Bartram was an Adam, collecting plants and naming them, who are we? While we busy ourselves making places, are we also inadvertently *unmaking* them? It has always been easy for me to make judgments about places, to draw a clear line between places I consider well-cared for or not, but at Maplehurst I have stumbled over my own pride and lost my grip on so many of my old convictions. The split-rail fences here at Maplehurst are smothered in wild grape vines threaded with poison ivy and brambles, proving that even home, the place we love more than any other, can have an untamable wilderness running through it.

We didn't wait long after my poison ivy began to heal to resume work on our patio. Despite the fact that it was now July in Virginia, the air felt fresh to us. We knew it was at least fifteen degrees hotter back in Texas, and our experience of weather is always as relative as it is objective. Our plan for the patio was simple: build a wooden frame, fill it with rubble and then sand, position our pavers, then fill in the gaps between them with more sand. I no longer remember the process itself, but I have never forgotten the moment when we first stepped back to survey our handiwork. Pleasure and pride bubbled up between us, until we noticed what we should have seen long before: our wooden frame was crooked. We could not purchase boards long enough for the full length, and so we had fitted together two shorter boards. Along the right side of the patio, the first board jutted out perpendicular from the wall, but the second, joined to it in order to continue that straight line, instead veered to the left. We had kept our noses so near to our task we were blinded to our obvious error.

❧

The wilderness is a place without paths. Its geography is unknown and unmapped. Wandering is what one does in the wilderness because nothing else is possible. To walk a straight path through the wilderness requires outside assistance, such as a pillar of fire—or GPS. If the metaphorical wilderness serves some purpose in our lives, that purpose is found primarily in waiting and in stillness. We may move in the wilderness, but we never arrive. Like the lines of our patio, we drift away from true, though in my experience such drifting often returns us to a deeper truth we could not have received before our wandering began.

In Virginia, unsure how to fill the time between college and the graduate program I dreamed of, I drifted into volunteer work with an adult education program run by one of the nuns at a nearby Benedictine monastery. When Sister Coleen retired from teaching, she single-handedly organized a volunteer-run tutoring program for English as a second language learners, those needing basic literacy skills, and adults studying for the high school equivalency exam. Sister Coleen was tiny, with skin and hair as papery and pale as the photocopied prayer books we used in the monastery chapel. Though the rules of the monastery had been relaxed after Vatican II, Sister Coleen still wore a modified habit of black skirt, white shirt, and the distinctive black-and-white veil. She told me she chose to dress like the nun she was because wherever she went out in the world, people in need felt comfortable approaching her. The veil was always slipping around on her head, but I never saw her without it. It was her welcome mat, the kind that normally sits outside a front door, but she took hers with her everywhere.

I began as a twice-a-week volunteer tutor, but within a few months I had joined Sister Coleen's tiny monastery office as a full-time staff member. My desk sat catty-corner to the desk of the only other employee. Maria, who was near my own age, had graduated from the local high school a few years before and was preparing her application to community college. She hoped to become a fully certified teacher. When she was only fourteen, an uncle had brought her to Virginia from her village in Mexico. I was twenty-one and had stepped into a Catholic church only twice in my life. Now Maria and I joined the sisters for prayer every day at noon sharp before eating lunch with Sister Coleen in the refectory.

The first trees I ever watched burn with autumn fire were trees planted by Benedictine nuns over a century and a half of caring for their rolling wooded property along a northern Virginia stream. Sister Coleen had lived most of her life among these trees, and she liked to introduce me to them, as if they were interesting friends with whom I had much in common. She pointed out that one of the first trees to lose its green in fall was the native dogwood. The small tree with the crispy brown leaves that clung to its branches all through the winter was a pin oak. The old leaves would only finally relinquish their hold on the slim branches when the new leaves arrived to push them out. The redbud trees that edged the woods like purple lace each spring were also called "Judas trees" because, according to the legend, Judas Iscariot, the traitor, had hung himself from the branches of just such a tree. It is said that the once-white blossoms of the tree blushed for shame. Others claim that the flowers of the redbud dangle like a hanging man. I have discovered those legends since, but I've never forgotten Sister Coleen's version: the limbs of these trees are weak so that the tree might never again carry such a shameful burden.

Sister Coleen was not one to recognize the boundary between professional life and personal life. She lived and worked within the context of place and community, and she assumed that I would too. When I asked for a day off because my mother was visiting from Texas, Sister Coleen insisted we both join her for noon prayer and lunch. When it was Sister Coleen's day to prepare the guest housing for monastery visitors, she asked me to set aside my office work to help. I followed her along winding paths carrying a stack of bath towels, still warm from the dryer. While she checked that the guest rooms were clean and well-stocked, I placed folded towels on the end of each bed. Sister Coleen did not know the guests who would stay in these rooms, and yet she prepared a place for them with great care. It seemed like the ideal kind of hospitality for an introvert like myself. Prepare a place, then step back and let the place itself be the welcome, the embrace, and the conversation. After that, when my mother came to stay, I also placed neatly folded towels, warm from the dryer, in a stack at the end of her bed.

Prepare a place, then step back and let the place itself be the welcome, the embrace, and the conversation.

Botanists have a word for the way some deciduous trees retain dead leaves through the winter: they call it *marcescence*. Marcescence is a potent trait, and it marks out certain trees, such as the pin oak, as halfway trees—neither fully evergreen nor fully deciduous. All trees shed dead leaves and needles. Pine trees and other evergreens do this continuously without ever emptying their branches entirely. Trees in the cherry family do it with drama and flourish, dropping yellowed leaves before summer is half over and standing bare by the time autumn finally arrives. But some trees defy tidy categories, and not even a proper, scientific term like *marcescence* can make them other than what they are: boundary trees and edge-dwellers whose true nature is revealed only on the threshold between winter and spring, when each new bud is sheltered and enclosed by the shell of last summer's leaf. Scientists have suggested that marcescence might signify more than an unfinished evolutionary phase. After all, those dead leaves on a pin oak keep hungry deer from dining on the tasty and tender new growth. The in-between can be purposeful. Sometimes, it is exactly what we need.

There's no denying the importance of the wilderness in the geography of faith. The Israelites became the Israelites in part through their wandering. Jesus took on the mantle of the Christ, the Messiah, through forty days in the wilderness. Every year, Christians around the world choose to reinhabit a kind of wilderness for the forty days of Lent. And God continues to lead each one of us in and out of wilderness places. Sometimes these wilderness places are metaphorical; sometimes they are places we can point to on a map.

The in-between can be purposeful. Sometimes, it is exactly what we need.

I have endured wilderness seasons, some brief, some terribly persistent, but only twice was the wilderness a place, and both times that place was beautiful. I thought Virginia was the most beautiful place I had ever lived, yet I struggled with loneliness and a sense that the work of my days required skills I simply didn't have. I felt as if I were only biding my time, waiting for life to carry me to some place where dreams—dreams of city life, dreams of travel, dreams of academic research—might be realized. On weekends, Jonathan and I went for long drives along country roads where green hills flowed into green mountains and fiery maples seemed to erupt with shouts of joy or defiance, depending on my own mood. Red apples and orange pumpkins teetered in precarious pyramids on farmstand tables where I bought a strange, new food called apple butter, and the sky was always cornflower blue. Perhaps it is a fool's errand, but I look back on those autumn days and search for some meaning in all that loveliness. Why was my wilderness so beautiful? Like the red and orange and yellow leaves themselves, did it signify? Was there some message to discern?

In those days, I did not listen for meaning, yet I found comfort in those first encounters with autumn beauty. Beauty couldn't fix my loneliness or alleviate the boredom that dropped like an anvil on my shoulders during the middle of a tutoring session so that I watched the clock with more misery than my hardworking students, but the beauty did offer escape and reprieve. It was cool water gushing from a desert rock, and Jonathan and I drank it in, putting mile after mile on our pickup truck. Things were better than they had been in Texas. "Look at those trees!" I exclaimed as we drove. And things were harder than Texas. "Christie," Jonathan said, "we can't travel home for Thanksgiving if we want to use my vacation days for Christmas." I did have two friends in Virginia, but they were different from me, and I often retreated from those differences. I felt as if I had taken a detour in life, and I was not sure I would ever find my way back to the main road.

Jonathan didn't feel perfectly at home in Virginia, as the suburbs had not figured in our dreams at all, but he at least had an absorbing new job. I, on the other hand, was surprised to learn that I could still feel homesick in a new and beautiful place. My homesickness was shot through with fear: *What if I never find a place where I can belong?* I had believed that our move to Virginia was a step toward happiness, and now I was unhappy in new ways. Yet dissatisfaction can sometimes be a gift. It can keep you dreaming, keep you seeking, keep you leaning forward into the future. The trick is that one day you'll have to learn to work through your discontentment without packing your boxes and moving on. In Virginia, I learned the necessary work of wandering as I waited for a path to some new place to reveal itself. Perhaps it is only now that I am learning the necessary work of staying put.

That first winter in Virginia, we played in the snow like children, and we borrowed our neighbor's snow shovel. In March, I saw my first electric-yellow forsythia shrub. I've never loved that vivid shade, but I turned my head and smiled every time I saw this new-to-me plant. That shrub was the living embodiment of a shout: *Spring is here!* One Saturday morning, Jonathan and I wandered beneath spring-blooming trees in Washington D.C. The famous cherry trees along the Tidal Basin frothed with blossom, as if we were all immersed in a foaming bubble bath, but something beyond their delicate branches, something more substantial and shaded a darker pink, caught my eye. Pushing my way through the crowds thronging the cherries, I found myself standing beneath a tree covered in pink flowers like tulips or enormous butterflies. I stood there long enough to decide that it looked like a tree covered in pink china teacups. But what could it be?

"It looks a little like a magnolia," I told Jonathan. "The flower petals are shaped like the leaves of the magnolia trees in Texas, but the flowers on those trees are big and white and surrounded by waxy green leaves. Those evergreens are nothing like this." A man standing nearby noticed my awe and confusion. "It's a northern magnolia," he said, "a saucer magnolia. Deciduous. If you like it, you should walk over to the Smithsonian Castle and visit the park behind."

What we found when we arrived was a small, grid-like park of squared paths interspersed with a dozen or so flowering trees just like the one we'd seen at the Tidal Basin. The park was hidden away behind the rust-red gothic stones of the Smithsonian Castle and delightfully free of crowds. Jonathan and I sat down on a bench and stared. I could not believe that such beautiful spring-blooming trees existed. I had never heard of them, never seen a picture. Even in Texas, I had learned about our capital's famous Japanese cherry blossoms. Why had I never been told about these? The joy of that first encounter was tempered by indignation, as if the most important thing in life is to tell others about all the beauty of the world, and someone had failed to tell me.

I want one, I thought. I had never wanted a tree of my own before, but now it was all I wanted. The thought of rising from that bench, returning to the car we'd parked at Union Station, and driving the long, straight highway west to a place with no tree in its postage stamp-sized front yard and only a crooked patio in the back seemed like returning to no home at all. *If we owned our own place, I could plant a saucer magnolia of my own. And I could choose a new color for the front door. And I could paint the ugly brown brick around the fireplace.* I was consumed with hunger for ownership. Startled by the beauty of spring, a beauty I had never known existed and so had never desired as I had desired the beauty of autumn leaves, I wanted to make this tree my own. I was waking up to the beauty of the natural world around me, but I thought in terms of control and consumption rather than responsibility. Perhaps I never have quite outgrown that way of thinking. I did not ask myself what it might require of me to belong to a place where such beauty could flourish, only whether it might be possible for such beauty to belong to me.

Sister Coleen loved the trees of her monastery home as if they were her friends, yet she knew, living in community as she did, that those trees did not belong to her. I see now that she knew she belonged to the trees, that she had some responsibility for them, and that she belonged to the One who had made them— and this is why she took such delight in them. Maria shared her delight. I remember how the two of them would exclaim over the darting movements of tiny chipmunks in the monastery garden or the delicate chirping of the birds that alighted on feeders just beyond our office window. When Sister Coleen sent me to the store with a list of needed office supplies, the first item on it was usually "birdseed."

Maria was rightly proud of the cozy, well-kept trailer home her boyfriend had given her, and she sometimes invited Sister Coleen and me to join her there for made-from-scratch rice flavored with tomato paste and studded with green peas and cubed carrots. That rice was a revelation to me, one that led me to ditch the boxed rice mixes I had been buying since college. Maria wanted to get married and have children, but the boyfriend's complicated tale of paperwork disappearing in Texas made me worry he already had a wife somewhere else. I couldn't understand why she put up with him, but I knew nothing of being young and alone in a country far from the one in which I had been born. I still know nothing of that, and I wish I had not lost touch with Maria. I wish I could sit on the soft banquette seat of her home and listen as she shares with me what her experience was really like.

I had chosen the halfway place I now called home, but I

would discover that Maria was stuck in a halfway place through no choice and no fault of her own. I was only a brief and imperfect witness to her life, but her friendship taught me that the sense of belonging I craved was also a privilege denied to some. Maria seemed to have no contact with family in Mexico, and she spoke of her village as if recalling a dream half-remembered. One afternoon, an administrator from the local community college called our office. He told Maria, with kindness, I suppose, that her application for financial aid had been quietly shredded. He thought she needed to know that the social security number she submitted with her paperwork belonged to someone else.

While Maria sat in her desk chair, tears streaming down her face, Sister Coleen quizzed her about her arrival in Virginia. Sister Coleen may have taken a vow of stability, but she knew far more about the world than either Maria or I. She held Maria's hand with a look on her face that suggested some part of her had known what was coming. But Maria was an innocent, and her shock was a terrible thing to see. As far as I understood, she never imagined that the papers her uncle had given her at age fourteen were anything but authentic.

I sat in my own desk chair making sympathetic noises and patting Maria's knee, but I felt as if I were watching someone die. We never talked again about college classes or her hope of becoming a teacher. The door to that future had slammed shut. Maria was stuck halfway between Mexico and Virginia, but hers wasn't a wilderness for wandering. Hers was for hiding. I no longer worried whether her boyfriend could marry her. I only hoped he'd help keep her safe.

> *In order to call a place our own, we inevitably lock others out. We say* mine *so much more easily than we say* ours.

It seemed that Virginia could never officially belong to Maria; she wasn't given legal status in the time we worked together, but now, all these years later and having lost touch with my friend, I wonder if she found some other way to belong to it. I wonder what words she would use to tell her own story of searching for home. I remember how she loved the birds and chipmunks and how she learned the English names for every unfamiliar tree. I like to think she did come to belong, though I do not know if she was able to stay. Virginia never belonged to me either, but the color of my skin and the official stamp on my birth certificate gave me the illusion, for a while, that it did. I see now that my investment in ownership emerged from a distorted view of belonging. I did not understand the many ways we can belong to a place without owning it. My mistake is a common one, and it is complicit in Maria's grief. In order to call a place our own, we inevitably lock others out. We say *mine* so much more easily than we say *ours*.

Is it possible to care for a place with open hands, always ready to give it away like so many fishes and loaves?

I resented my status as renter. I resented the tedious, empty space between my finished past and my dreamed-of future. I imagined I would feel more fulfilled, more at home, if we owned our own place, but I was so blinded by some far-off vision, I failed to notice the poison ivy or the crooked line of our patio or all the ways we deny others the very things we want most for ourselves. The places we call home sometimes need protection from our inexperience and our selfishness. The places we call home are almost always enriched to the extent that they are shared. Is it possible to care for a place without hurting it, through ignorance or arrogance? Is it possible to care for a place with open hands, always ready to give it away like so many fishes and loaves?

According to Sister Coleen, the redbuds, those Judas trees that lined the roads with purple each spring, made themselves weak-limbed in order to shrug off the burden of shame Judas laid on them. In a way, the redbuds of legend unmade themselves. Having learned that strength left them vulnerable to misuse, they chose weakness. In similar ways, my Virginia home began the process of unmaking me. Beneath autumn leaves and spring blossoms, I made mistakes and bumped up, hard, against limitations. My confident sense that I could improve any place was shaken just enough to humble me and make me receptive to a truth I am still learning: *placemaking has more to do with growing smaller and weaker than it does with control or ownership.* When we release our grip on ownership and consent to be small, we create space—for trees, for animals, for other people. Scripture only hints at Judas's last days, and the historical truth is now embroidered with many legends, but we know at least that those thirty pieces of silver went toward the purchase of a field that would be called, for many generations, the "Field of Blood." The silver and the land were tainted by association with treachery. But if the redbuds found redemption in their delicate springtime beauty, the field found its own redemption by making space for the foreigner. In time, the Field of Blood was dedicated as a burial place for non-Israelites.

Placemaking has more to do with growing smaller and weaker than it does with control or ownership.

I had dreamed of autumn trees for most of my life, but the unexpected beauty of the spring trees was one of the sweetest and least anticipated gifts I was given in Virginia. Before Virginia, I had not known that the prize for enduring a real winter, with its occasional wonderland days and its regular misery days, was an awakening so astonishing it felt as if I learned what the word *spring* meant for the first time in my life. Spring wasn't simply a pleasant interlude; it wasn't merely the chance to catch one's breath between the ice storm and the heat wave. It was a fulfillment. It was a promise kept, though I had not even realized a promise had been made. Like winter, the wilderness is always a promise. God leads us in and, one way or another, he leads us out again. Or, if he doesn't lead us out, he does something almost more miraculous: he plants trees in the desert, and he causes rivers to flow there.

Like winter, the wilderness is always a promise. God leads us in and, one way or another, he leads us out again. Or, if he doesn't lead us out, he does something almost more miraculous: he plants trees in the desert, and he causes rivers to flow there.

The promises named in the book of Isaiah are more beautiful than anything I've discovered in the tree encyclopedia I love so much: "I, the God of Israel, . . . will make rivers flow on barren heights . . . I will put in the desert the cedar and the acacia, the myrtle and the olive. I will set junipers in the wasteland, the fir and the cypress together."[5] In my Bible, I have listed out the trees and plants I encountered during my first, brief sojourn in the wilderness: saucer magnolia, eastern redbud, pin oak, dogwood, and forsythia, bright as any guiding light.

The wilderness is not necessarily a desolate place. It has its own unique beauty, and that beauty is enough. It does not need us. It does not ask for our participation. This may be one reason why wilderness wandering is such a harsh experience, but this is certainly one reason why time in the wilderness is a gift. Our cultivation and our care are not required. God himself plants trees in that place; God himself draws water from dry rocks. The gift of the wilderness is that this is the place we go simply to receive. This is the place we go to listen. In the wilderness, we are given the opportunity to lay down the burden of our desire to make and remake so that when some other place invites our participation and our creative efforts, we are ready to offer those things with humility. The trees—even in the wilderness—are singing a song, but if we plunge ahead in accompaniment without first stopping to listen,

In the wilderness, we are given the opportunity to lay down the burden of our desire to make and remake so that when some other place invites our participation and our creative efforts, we are ready to offer those things with humility.

and without letting ourselves be changed by the song, we may find ourselves leaving not beauty but crooked patios and poison ivy and heartbroken tears in our wake.

Chapter 4

Honey Locust

GAINING AND LOSING
THE CITY

S ome trees cast dappled shade and some trees cast hardly any shade at all, but a few trees blanket their circumference in shade so complete that stepping beneath their branches is like stepping into a stone church and shutting a heavy door behind you. The door closes with a gentle thud, and you are enclosed in cool quiet. My tree encyclopedia calls the shade cast by these trees "dense" and warns against the futile hope that sun-loving grass or even shade-loving hostas might grow beneath them. From the time I was a child seeking out hiding places beneath tables and tucked up on branches, I have loved these deep-shade trees best of all. By limiting and defining space, they somehow make more room for the inner life of reflection and imagination. They are a world within a world.

We moved into Maplehurst on the first day of August. That afternoon, I stood beneath the dense canopy of the largest

Magnolia soulangeana, or saucer magnolia, I had ever seen. The tree was a great umbrella above me, and sunlight caused the green silk of the leaves to glow. The tree was planted perhaps twenty yards from the white spindles of our new front porch. I struggled to imagine what this tree might look like in spring. It was twice as tall and three times as wide as the magnolias I'd seen growing behind the Smithsonian Castle thirteen years before. The tree felt like a promise, one I did not yet have the faith to believe. That August, I was weighed down by a yet-to-be-born baby girl and surrounded by more anxieties than moving boxes. *Would my mother-in-law arrive in time for the birth? Would I ever find the box of baby clothes? Could Jonathan begin a new job and still find time to mow five acres of grass?* Eight months later, the boxes were unpacked, the anxieties had dissipated, and the promise was fulfilled. In April, I lay on my back on a blanket beneath that tree. Pink tulip flowers danced against an impossibly blue sky while my baby daughter clapped her hands and laughed.

For several spring seasons in a row, this magnolia has been a sentinel, the custodian of spring's arrival. Spring-blooming magnolias are susceptible to late frosts, and whenever the tree begins to bloom, checking the daily weather forecasts becomes an obsessive habit. A sudden drop in temperature, so common in early spring, can turn the blossoms from gorgeous porcelain tea-cups to unappealing blobs of tissue. Sometimes our tree blooms in March, sometimes in April, but every spring until this one, it has bloomed. This spring at Maplehurst was one for the record books. "The warmest February ever recorded," the newspaper said. Warm enough to fool the magnolia tree, despite its great age and deep roots and long experience with the vagaries of winter winds. Toward the end of February, I noticed a haze of pink above the chicken coop. *No, please no,* I thought. Stepping beneath the shelter of the magnolia's bare, gray branches, I saw that every bud on every branch had cracked open its fuzzy protective shell, and a thousand or more pink petals were peeking out at a winter sky. The vulnerability of those tissue paper petals took my breath away.

If February was especially balmy, March was unusually bitter. One morning, ice coated the pale blossoms of our apricot tree, and I knew we'd have no apricots that year. Another morning, we woke to ten inches of heavy, sloppy snow. The kids yelped with pleasure and gathered up their sleds, but I worried for the early yellow daffodils. *Would the snow insulate them or would it crush them?* And through it all, I hoped the magnolia tree might still have at least a few of its buds held in reserve for the day spring arrived to stay. The snow melted, the weather warmed, and the yellow daffodils bounced back. Even ten inches of snow was no match for their cheerful perseverance. But the magnolia skipped spring entirely and shifted right into summer. Soon, the mushy brown flower buds were replaced by summer's green leaves.

This year, it feels as if everything that once seemed steadfast and reliable here at Maplehurst is deteriorating, even the seasons themselves. I never imagined my favorite spring moments could crumble away like peeling paint or limestone mortar. And yet what, really, have I lost? Not food for my children. Not a field of cotton, peanuts, or watermelon, as my grandfather may have known. Only beauty. But it is the beauty particular to this place, and that makes it precious and irreplaceable.

At the beginning of our second spring in Virginia, I flew on my own to Chicago for a graduate student open house, my nervous excitement matching the gentle turbulence of the plane. I had almost decided to accept admission to a PhD program offered to me by the English department at the University of Chicago, but since neither Jonathan nor I had ever been to Chicago, I needed to see it for myself. What I saw on campus that cold, early spring weekend were solitary students bundled against the wind and immense walls of gray Gothic stone the same muted color as the sky. The only visible warmth came from the rosy-pink butterfly flowers on a row of blooming saucer magnolias. Standing alone on a quiet sidewalk, I gazed at those flowers. It was the moment I first believed this strange and unfamiliar environment might one day feel like home.

In order to gain the city, we had to lose square footage in the suburbs. Our Virginia townhouse had one master bedroom, one small bedroom for guests, and one even smaller bedroom for our computer and desk. But on the bus ride from the University of Chicago's campus to the airport at the end of my department open house weekend, I had glimpsed the curved façade of an elegant stone apartment building. It faced the open park around the Museum of Science and Industry, and the green copper dome of its entrance looked out over the sands of 57th Street Beach and the freshwater waves of Lake Michigan. While the bus idled at a red light, I caught the name on a shiny brass plaque: *The Windermere.*

I had seen no more of the building than I had once seen of my great-grandfather's orchard of pecan trees, but since then I had, at least, learned the importance of a passing glance. Back in Virginia with Jonathan, we called the apartment manager's office at the Windermere. She told us the only apartment available for rent that summer was a tiny one-bedroom unit on the third floor facing the museum. "We'll take it!" we told her. And then we took a good look at our furniture. We hadn't accumulated much in the past two years, but we'd have to let go of our guest bed, a spare sofa, and perhaps even our microwave. We would need to sell our Texas truck. We would need to buy warmer coats. If family came to visit us in our new home, we would give them our bed. We could always buy an air mattress. Downsizing felt like an adventure, a small price to pay to realize our dream of high-rise city living.

Built in the 1920s as a ritzy, waterfront apartment hotel, the Windermere had an atmosphere I loved at first sight. It was rumored that Al Capone once owned a speakeasy in the subterranean tunnel that connected the building with an underground parking garage, and I could easily imagine the mirrored back wall of the elevator reflecting flappers in fur coats as well as the glossy wood paneling and shiny brass handrail. Crystal ceiling lights sparkled down the length of each long hallway. Our apartment was small, but the ceilings soared and the plaster moldings looked like frosting on an architectural wedding cake. Directly across the narrow street, and visible from every one of our few windows, was a small strip of parkland between our building and the museum beyond. Tall trees with wispy, delicate leaves grew there.

I remember those trees with gratitude. I had been dreaming of the city for years, and my dream was coming true in the form of old brick, slate sidewalks, and elevated trains. And yet it would be the many trees in this neighborhood that would enable me to feel at home in this place for so long. Occasionally, in those years, I would visit friends in other parts of the city. It was in those neighborhoods without trees—where the only gardens were inaccessible rooftop plots—that I began to recognize how much of my love for the city I owed to the hospitable corners, pockets, and ribbons of flowing water and green, growing things.

The extensive park system in our neighborhood didn't happen by accident. It was the desire and design of the neighborhood's founder, Paul Cornell. When he first acquired this land south of the city in 1853, he announced his ambitions by naming it for London's celebrated Hyde Park. Later, he hired the famous landscape architect Frederick Law Olmsted to design the extensive green spaces on the neighborhood's borders. In a city, trees are not a given. They must be planned for and cared for, and Cornell is remembered and honored for doing exactly that. In Chicago's Hyde Park neighborhood, I could step beneath the branches of a tree and shut out the city. It was a world within a world.

A friend once emailed me a photograph of a blooming saucer magnolia with the comment, "Isn't our Creator marvelous?" I appreciated that she had remembered my love for this tree, and I replied simply, *Yes*. What I thought, however, was this: *If* Magnolia soulangeana *is a hybrid tree, does that make a human being, rather than God, its creator?* I once joked with another friend that while God may have created mauve and mustard flowers, it was the horticulturists who created pretty ones. While it is true that wild zinnias are mustard yellow and wild gladiolas tend toward muddy mauve, nearly all the colors of the rainbow are locked up inside their genes. And human intervention isn't always required for hybridization. The magic of spontaneous hybridization occurs frequently in nature, for instance, when two wild roses with single flowers cross-pollinate and create a new rose with scented double blooms. Creating hybrids of some plants is so easy that anyone with two daffodils or two daylilies in the backyard can try their hand at creating an entirely new flower. Our Maker has made it easy for us to follow in his creative footsteps. Still, most of our favorite hybrid trees and garden plants are the work of dedicated plant breeders who carefully hand pollinate and sow seed after seed in pursuit of the blue rose or the re-blooming peony, or some lovely tree or flower no one has ever seen before.

The saucer magnolia was created by Étienne Soulange-Bodin, a former French soldier who had traveled and battled across Europe in Napoleon's army. He once wrote that French soldiers had camped in German gardens and German soldiers had camped in French gardens, and both would have been better off staying home to plant cabbages. Soulange-Bodin quite literally hammered his sword into a plowshare when he retired from soldiering. He opened an exotic plant nursery outside Paris and eventually became one of France's most respected horticulturalists. Soulange-Bodin had two magnolias growing in his nursery, both introduced from China. One, *Magnolia liliiflora*, had a lovely shape and white flowers. The other, *Magnolia denudata*, was shrubby, but its flowers were shot through with purple. Hoping to create a new tree with the most desirable traits of each, Soulange-Bodin crossed the two varieties by hand, and sometime around 1820, the saucer magnolia was born with both a graceful shape and brightly colored flowers.[1]

I know the *Magnolia soulangeana* well. It has been a beacon to me. But its two wild parent trees, the magnolias that grew in China before traveling to that Paris nursery, are to me only names in a book. I have never seen one growing in a yard or a park. The world's love for the saucer magnolia has crowded out the affection we once had for her parent trees. They are lost to the world I inhabit and can be found only in my gardening books and internet searches. Soulange-Boudin wrote that *Magnolia liliiflora* had purple flowers, but I wonder if I would call them pink? The white blooms of *Magnolia denudata* are said to resemble lilies. I stare at images online and try to decide if the flowers are cup-like. Or do they have recurved petals rolling back like curls of white chocolate as so many wild lilies do? I suppose the question I am really asking is this: How much does humanity's making depend upon loss? Is our "one art" always the "art of losing," as one of my favorite poets claims?[2]

Loving someone enlarges your sense of what is beautiful. I never gave freckles much thought, but the freckles on my older son's nose are so sweetly beautiful to me I once tried to count them. As I learned to love our new home in the city, my eyes opened to beauty that had once been beyond my reckoning. When I visited Chicago that open-house weekend, I noticed but avoided venturing through the tunnel-like viaducts that ran beneath the tracks of an elevated train. They were dark and damp and splashed with graffiti, and I did not trust them. *Where could they possibly lead?* I discovered the answer only after we moved. Each little wilderness of dark viaduct eventually opened out onto green spaces and blue water so endless it might have been the ocean.

Nearly all places on our planet are made or shaped in some sense. Agriculture shapes the course of rivers and logging changes the forest, but the city is a made environment in almost every way. In a city, it is more difficult to imagine that the ground beneath your feet belongs to you, even if your name is on the deed. In a city, we see more clearly that placemaking occurs in the context of community, and the care of a place is a shared respon-sibility. On the south side of Chicago, the history of everything from race relations and the Great Migration to the music of the blues is laid out like a grid of city streets. In my new home, I was caught up in a fascinating maze of history I had never learned. I had washed my walls in blue paint before I understood that the square cupboards lining the wall above our closet were sized precisely to hold an elegant lady's fashionable hatboxes. I filled those square spaces with photograph albums, the dried flowers of my wedding bouquet, and the pump for our new air mattress.

In a city, we see more clearly that placemaking occurs in the context of community, and the care of a place is a shared responsibility.

Lately, I've been sitting on the front porch at Maplehurst reading a book about forests, and I've decided that a forest ecosystem is a lot like a city. Apparently certain trees, such as the oak and beech and spruce, were never meant to grow alone. We are just beginning to learn how deeply social trees can be, and many traditional notions about "managing" a healthy forest now seem self-defeating or even harmful. In my book, the German forester Peter Wohlleben writes of discovering a circle of mossy stones in a preserve of old beech trees.[3] The stones were such an unusual shape—gently curved and hollowed out in places—that Wohlleben lifted some of the moss to study their shape more closely. Beneath the moss he found not stone but tree bark. He realized then that he was surrounded by the remains of a giant beech tree. The center of the stump had long ago rotted away, leaving only the mossy, weathered rim. Because the heart of the stump had completely transformed into humus for the forest floor, Wohlleben judged that the tree had died at least four or five hundred years before. But why did the rim of the stump still appear so solid?

Wohlleben tried to shift the wood, but it wouldn't move. Clearly, it was still rooted, somehow, into the earth. Curious, he used a pocketknife to remove more moss and a little of the old bark. Beneath the blade of his knife, he found not soft, decaying wood as he expected, but a flash of vivid green. Green: the color of chlorophyll. Chlorophyll gives new leaves their color, and it is stored in the trunks of living trees. This wood, stone-like, rooted, and covered in soft moss, was still alive. It had no leaves to capture sunlight and make chlorophyll through photosynthesis. No tree can starve for hundreds of years and remain green and alive in its core. The only explanation was that the surrounding beech trees were somehow feeding the roots of this stump. But how? And why?

Scientists have looked into similar forest scenarios and determined that neighboring trees can feed the remains of other trees remotely, through fungal connections between roots or directly through the roots themselves. Other scientists have concluded that not only are the roots of trees in undisturbed forests connected, but the trees are able to distinguish between their own roots, the roots of other trees of the same species, and the roots of non-related trees. The picture that has emerged is far more complex than roots growing chaotically and simply bumping into one another. Something like that does appear to happen in planted forests where the roots of nursery trees have been pruned and roughly handled before transplantation. Those trees, perhaps because of damage to their roots, seem to live for themselves. But true forest trees, like city dwellers or members of a tribe, appear to understand that they are stronger together. A tree within a forest is included in a special, protective ecosystem. Nearby are other trees who will feed it in times of injury or sickness and help buffer it in storms. Forest trees are united in maintaining the forest canopy; it is their shared shelter from summer heat and winter squalls. The trees know what we struggle to accept: it is right and good to love my neighbor as myself. My fate, and my neighbor's fate, are bound up together. No human and no tree is an island.

Today, some well-meaning placemaker, perhaps a forester or a gardener, is cutting down a tree, mistakenly supposing she is giving the other trees a little more sunlight and some much-needed elbow room. Today, I am staring at that spot where Beau and I wanted an oak tree to grow and wondering if those acorns knew something I didn't. Is a single oak tree on someone's front lawn an image of abundance or an image of scarcity? Is a single oak tree an exile? If so, the white oak on the golf course is the king of exiles, standing alone near the edge of that too-green turf, the last living member of its birthright forest. Recently, I found an online database for Pennsylvania's oldest trees and discovered justification for my concerns about that oak on the golf course. Because of its size, it is mentioned near the top of the list. It was last measured in 2010, two years before our arrival at Maplehurst and thirteen years after the golf course was built. It is one of the oldest white oaks in the state, and the website's description of it is sobering. "In bad shape," it reads. "Not likely to survive damage from golf course construction."

An apartment building is a world within a world, but those worlds are interdependent. At the Windermere, I found it easy to love the crystal pendant lights in the building's hallways and the aged brass of the antique letter box in the lobby, but the enclosed world also included dangers, such as the neighbor who once fell asleep with a cigarette in his hand. The small fire in his apartment could have spread; it could have swept us up as well, like a forest fire. Proximity is risky. And yet our neighbors also supported us, delighted us, inspired us, needed us.

Across the hall were two Juilliard-trained musicians. She was American, he was French, and their small son sometimes dashed up and down the carpeted hallway in navy blue rain boots. "Pierre! Pierre!" his mother would call, and I would peek around my door, hoping to catch a glimpse of this adorable little boy. A few years after we left the Windermere, I read about the French violinist's promotion to first chair in the Chicago Symphony Orchestra, but all I could remember of him was the day when a dozen neighbors gathered for brunch. "Where is your husband?" we asked Pierre's mother. "Oh, he's back in our apartment with his parents," she said. "They're visiting from Paris. At noon they'll sit down for roast beef and red wine like they always do." I nodded, my eyes wide. Apparently, the French didn't believe in brunch.

That morning, we ate bacon glazed with maple syrup and scrambled eggs cooked with a touch of cream cheese and fresh chives, all made by another neighbor named Eva. She was a personal chef and caterer and cooked far above us in her kitchen on the twelfth floor. From Eva, I learned that simple, familiar cooking is the most hospitable, but even ordinary foods can be made extraordinary with an extra ingredient or two. All these years later, if Jonathan and I make a special breakfast, we gently scramble eggs with cream cheese before topping them with fresh, chopped chives. That morning, seated with another couple around the coffee table, we exclaimed over the bacon and eggs. He was American and working on a combined PhD / MD. She was Danish and finishing her PhD. She looked exactly like my mental image of a Dane: tall and strong with long, blonde braids. They had a baby boy, Patrick, with the roundest, sweetest face I had ever seen. After that brunch, we sometimes watched Patrick while his parents ran errands. I remember Jonathan and I passing that happy, laughing baby between us and wondering if we would ever create such a marvel.

Then, I lived in a city building as full of humanity as a forest is full of trees. Now I live in a crumbling farmhouse set apart on a hill. I no longer linger in the hallway while my neighbor Claudia tells me about her day and complains about the woman on duty at the front door. "Is it really so hard to smile?" she would say. "I dread asking her for my packages!" And I am no longer visited by Carmen, one of the apartment managers, herself a resident of the seventh floor, who asked my opinion of the carpet and wallpaper she chose for the building's redecoration. The wallpaper was a swirl of rich blues and greens, and I told her the truth. "It's perfect. It's beautiful. It's just what I would choose."

I still have a relic of those Windermere days. Downstairs, in the room with the fieldstone fireplace that we call the parlor (because the previous owners called it that before us), sits a square, wooden table. The top was once leather, though most of the leather has worn away. Clearly, it was originally meant for playing cards, perhaps after dinner, and that is often what we use it for today, though I imagine the first owners played bridge or canasta rather than Uno. I have the table because one afternoon, Carmen knocked on our door and suggested we might want to run up to the twelfth floor. One of the building's oldest residents had recently died, and his family was cleaning out his rooms. This man had lived in the Windermere since he was a little boy and the building had been a furnished hotel. His apartment still contained some of the original furnishings. I was busy with classwork, but Jonathan followed Carmen to the elevator. He returned not long after, squeezing the table through our door and telling me all about the views of Lake Michigan from that twelfth-floor apartment. The twelfth floor felt like a different world from the third, he said. Now, when I run my hands across the old, scarred leather of our Windermere inheritance, I imagine worlds within worlds within worlds.

In the city, home is never a clean slate. It is always something inherited, something handed on from one generation to the next, one neighbor to another. I can only imagine how many layers of paint there were on those hatbox cupboards. At the Windermere, our home was the human equivalent of a cell in a beehive or a tree in a forest. Jonathan and I were a part of a community, and that knowledge changed our attitude toward home in subtle ways. If I wanted to hammer a nail into the wall in order to hang a framed photograph, I thought about whether Patrick or Pierre might be napping, and I thought about Jeff the custodian, who had been such a help when we first moved in. One day, he might be the one filling this hole in order to repaint the wall. Jonathan and I no longer hammered nails with careless abandon, but in a transient world of short-term leases for students who came and went, even our small placemaking efforts meant more. Covering the landlord's white walls with a beautiful paint color was so unusual (*Why spend anything extra from a small graduate student stipend? Why bother when graduation is six months away?*) that everyone who entered our small apartment smiled with surprise and delight.

An inherited home might be a burden in some ways, but it is also a gift. At the Windermere, Jonathan and I could belong to Chicago because we were responsible for a small part of it. We belonged to the city's rich history. We belonged to our neighbors and to the lake and to the big, imposing museum across the street.

We belonged to a place that was beautiful but also in need, here and there, of regeneration. Some spot was always being made better, and some other spot was always falling apart. We needed to be surprised by how much we enjoyed a baby's round cheeks, and we needed to draw near to poverty through the homeless men and women who called our shared streets home. Some of these men and women became friends, like Walter and Jessica, who always helped us lay out coffee and donuts on a long table outside the neighborhood club gymnasium where our church held Sunday morning services. I don't know if we needed the family-owned Italian restaurant on the first floor, but the salad of olive oil-packed tuna, sundried tomatoes, and baby spinach I could pick up quickly from their deli counter before heading to class was also a gift. We loved the green patina on our building's copper dome, and we learned to love the rainbow-colored graffiti on the viaduct down the street.

We needed this place, and this place needed us, at least a little bit. It needed us to help make it and to make it better, but before we could even begin to do that, it needed us to see it and to learn its names. First, I learned street names (and numbers). Our new world was bounded by 47th Street on the north and 61st Street on the south. Odd-numbered streets were mostly commercial. That's where we went for books and pizza and Thai food. Even-numbered streets were mostly residential. That's where we went for church small group or a graduate student party. Next, I learned neighborhood names, such as Hyde Park and Kenwood and Woodlawn. Only much later did I learn to name the trees that gave those neighborhood names their meaning.

I made quite a few friends that first year among my cohort of PhD students, but one of my favorites was Matteo. He was older than Jonathan and I were and lived with his girlfriend in an apartment crowded with one thousand books. On my first visit to his home, he gave me a tour of his bookshelves, served me peppermint tea, and sent me home with a vintage desk lamp he had rescued from a trash heap. The lamp had a small, old-fashioned plug and art deco flourishes on its molded Bakelite base. It was just the right size for my Windermere card table. One sunny afternoon, I bumped into Matteo on the sidewalk somewhere between campus and my apartment. He had a book in his hands, and he was peering into the shaded corners of a small courtyard garden. After we said hello, he explained that he had been trying to learn the name of every tree in our neighborhood. "That," he said pointing to a tree in the courtyard, "is an eastern redbud. Can you see the heart-shaped leaves?"

I knew the redbud from our time in Virginia, yet it had not occurred to me that the trees in my new city home were worth my time and attention. I had forgotten or perhaps learned only incompletely Sister Coleen's lesson, which is also the lesson of the poets: "To name is to know and remember."[4] Matteo was a poet, but like me and our fellow students, he was also an academic in training. In the library or department lounge, we buried our noses in books. Around the seminar table, we tried to sound more sophisticated and intelligent than we felt. Every scrap of knowledge we gleaned was to be used—in our papers, in our conversations with faculty during department sherry parties, even in our conversations with one another at the university pub late at night. Knowledge was a crutch, a shield, sometimes a weapon. Tree knowledge was of no use to me here, and so I had never even considered it. But when Matteo pointed out the redbud on the corner, I realized how different he was from the rest of us. Unlike me, he had never lost sight of the world outside our university quadrangle. "Will you teach me too?" I asked.

❧

I remember the name of only one tree I learned on that walk with Matteo. *Honey locust.* When I think of my old Chicago neighborhood, it is the honey locust trees that come to mind, even before I remember the Frank Lloyd Wright homes or the neo-gothic quadrangles draped every autumn in blood-red Boston ivy. Honey locusts lined most of the streets I walked on a daily basis, and I often kicked up the long, dusty seedpods they dropped all over the cracked, slate sidewalks in late fall. The pulp inside is supposedly quite sweet and was a food for the native peoples who first belonged to this place and called it home. Michael Dirr tells me the thornless common honey locust is a popular street tree in the Midwest. He also tells me what I already know and will never forget: these trees have "a delicate and sophisticated silhouette," and the fine, feathery foliage turns a "rich golden yellow" in the fall.[5] But Dirr's encyclopedia also reminds me of something I had forgotten or perhaps failed to notice: the feather-like leaves of this tree cast such a light shade that grass is able to grow right up and around the trunk. In this, they are quite unlike my beloved saucer magnolia. They do not shut out the larger world; they adorn it. Perhaps it is no wonder my Chicago memories are all edged with lacy, golden leaves.

There are no honey locust trees at Maplehurst. In my mind, they belong only to Chicago, which makes my memory of them bittersweet since I no longer belong to that city myself. Sometimes people visit us here at Maplehurst and say, "Look at where life has brought you! How lucky you are." And I smile and nod and acknowledge my gratitude for this Pennsylvania farmhouse. But what I cannot explain, at least not without appearing ungrateful, is that we do not have some American dream of trading up for bigger and better. Or, if we have, it is in appearance only, not substance. Despite the cultural messages of our home-buying television shows and home decorating magazines, excess square footage is more likely to be a burden than a refuge. This old farmhouse and these five acres of land, impressive as they may be, are not really more valuable than our 400 square feet at the Windermere. We are placemakers on a bigger scale now, and the burdens and the joys have grown with the responsibilities. But our "trading up" has involved loss as well as gain. I still long for the honey locust trees, though I am longing for the city friends I would run into at the park and the city blocks where I pushed three precious babies in strollers as much as I long for the yellow leaves like feathers underfoot.

Here at Maplehurst, I use one of the third-floor rooms with sloping ceilings as an office. In this room, there are two small, arched windows facing north down the long driveway. One is filled with the green leaves of our majestic magnolia. From my desk, I can see the mystery I first noticed last night from the front porch. Our magnolia tree, though it did not bloom in spring, is now covered with flowers. This tree has always thrown out the occasional summer bloom but nothing like this. This year, it has become something it has never been before: a summer-flowering wonder, a green globe dotted all over with pale-pink flowers. At least, they appear pink in daylight. But yesterday, as the light dimmed toward evening, they began to glow. The tree's dark green leaves faded into the general darkness, but the flowers became brighter and brighter until they looked like stars coming out one by one. My tree books say nothing about this, and even the internet is no help. I have only my own observation to suggest that this tree, because it lost every one of its spring blossoms, is now determined to flower and set seed in summer. Like Maplehurst itself, this is a gift only loss could give.

I have lost Chicago and no longer call that city home, but what gifts did I receive in the living, the loving, *and* the losing? I am more aware of the nearness of my neighbors. I may not be able to see my neighbors down around a bend in this country road, but I couldn't see my neighbors on the twelfth floor, either. We may feel ourselves to live in a small world, deeply shaded and isolated, but there is a path between every pair of front doors, no matter how long the distance between them, and my placemaking choices can impact many. Chicago also proved to me that it is possible to feel deeply at home in this world. Hyde Park wasn't a perfect place, and we rarely, if ever, felt perfectly happy, perfectly safe, or perfectly comfortable there, but our delight in our surroundings was matched by an assurance that we were living our lives exactly where we were meant to be living them. I feel a similar sense of belonging here at Maplehurst, but it is shaded by longing for the particular beauties of a place I no longer call home. I wonder if loving and losing a place causes our hearts to fracture. Or does it enlarge our capacity for loving and making some other place well? Placemaking asks that we love a place with all of ourselves, but placemakers don't always get to stay in the places they have made. Placemaking offers no protection from all the many forms loss can take.

Am I brave enough to risk my heart again?

Placemaking asks that we love a place with all of ourselves, but placemakers don't always get to stay in the places they have made. Placemaking offers no protection from all the many forms loss can take.

Chapter 5

Penn's Woods

THE ABUNDANCE OF EMPTY PLACES

Who are the placemakers? They are often the ones who look like fools. They follow extravagant and impractical dreams. They sometimes waste their time and their money, and though they work hard, others often consider them unproductive. While the world races past on smooth concrete, they patiently tend soil with a yearly application of chopped leaves and the clearings from the henhouse. They plant trees they will never live to see full-grown. They know the names and the histories of the antique roses. They keep garbage bags in the trunk of their car, and they are not afraid to stop near rushing traffic to gather beer cans, water bottles, and plastic shopping bags. I never saw myself as one of them. "Tree hugger" was not an identity I aimed for, yet I look back and see a steady progression toward a way of life I might once have thought mad. Though we spent seven years caring for a city garden that would one day eventually be erased by an excavator, today I say with complete sincerity, *It was worthwhile.*

Gain precedes loss, and loss precedes restoration, but most stories begin even before that; most stories begin with emptiness. At the beginning of all things, the earth was formless and empty. At the beginning of our marriage, my womb was empty, and for six years it remained so. We planted our first garden while we were still living at the Windermere, and it grew in a vacant city lot surrounded by cracked sidewalks, industrial chimneys, and anonymous brick apartment buildings. On the exact line where the University of Chicago met the Woodlawn neighborhood, a small and shifting community of placemakers cultivated emptiness in order to harvest tomatoes, basil, garlic, berries, and so much else. Someone had an idea for a community bread oven, and someone else built it. Lush green vines were envisioned, then planted, and they grew over an arbor to shade our shared picnic table. This South Side community garden wasn't a perfect paradise. A fellow gardener, or perhaps a neighborhood wanderer, did steal our one and only cantaloupe just before we planned to pick it ourselves, but the ground of that garden was more fertile for friendships and homemade pesto and even our marriage than any place we had yet known. Our family grew from two to three while digging in that dirt.

Today, at Maplehurst, I am daily distracted by the large empty space beyond our front door. Of course, empty is in the eye of the beholder. The space is spread with the grass and weeds we call a lawn, and it is anchored by the remains of two enormous tree stumps. Maples, I assume. But to me, it is a space that appears empty, a void in the landscape. We already have a fenced-in vegetable garden on the other side of the house, but I wonder if I dare make a flower garden here, in this prominent spot where mistakes cannot be hidden. If I do, the garden will begin with more emptiness. The stumps must be dug out with specialized machinery, the grass sliced out with my spade. But when I sit on the black wicker glider on the wraparound porch near the front door, I imagine I am gazing out at a formal garden with a vine-covered arch at its entrance and four quadrants divided by paths around a central, circular bed, like four spokes on a flowery wheel. I can almost see a potting shed in the back, with cedar shingles on its pointed roof, and beds overfull with the flowers I know I'll love even though I have never grown them: roses, my father's favorite irises, and lilies tall and heavy with the weight of their own perfume. Lilies just like the ones I used to buy from a flower grower at the Hyde Park Farmers Market on 53rd Street.

How can I justify the expense of time, money, and effort for flowers, especially when the house needs so much? The type of garden shed I have in mind is often called a "folly" in my English gardening books. The name is probably apt, and I should shut my eyes, walk away, and forget all about this foolish vision. Yet I know myself well enough by now to accept that even if I shut them, my eyes will always seek out the possibility in empty places. Who are the placemakers? They are the ones who gaze out over emptiness and, sometimes through tears, see shimmering possibility.

My children, like most Pennsylvania schoolchildren, will tell you that our state is named for its founder, William Penn. But history tells a more complicated tale. Penn once studied maps of this land and saw both the possibilities of an empty place and the reminders of a place he already knew and loved. Penn first intended to name the land west of the Delaware River "New Wales" because descriptions he had read suggested it resembled the rolling green hills of his beloved Welsh countryside.[1] When King Charles II disapproved, Penn suggested "Sylvania," a fanciful word related to the Latin for "trees" or "forest." Penn was dismayed when the king insisted on prepending the name "Penn" in memory of his friend, William's father. Penn worried the name would seem vain, but he comforted himself with the thought that in Welsh, "Penn" refers to a high place. Today, most residents of Pennsylvania translate our state's name as "Penn's Woods," but to William Penn himself, Pennsylvania always meant "high woodland." Almost 250 years later, remnants of that same woodland, like the Penn Oak on the golf course behind my house, still breathe for me and my neighbors, still honor both a visionary placemaker and his father. Place names are layered with meaning, almost as if they sought to mimic the layers of rock and sediment in the land itself.

Emptiness is certainly in the eye of the beholder, and the high woodland I now call home was in Penn's day already the home of the Lenni Lenape tribe. The Lenni Lenape hunted, fished, and farmed what one of my local history books calls this "productive wilderness," a phrase that seems to mean far more than I can yet articulate.[2] If the European colonists came to clear land and plant orchards, did they make the land more or less productive than it already was? Perhaps productivity is also in the eye of the beholder.

In 1700, an English Quaker named George Peirce purchased land for a farm from William Penn. That 402-acre tract of land lies approximately ten miles east and just slightly north of Maplehurst. In 1709, George's son Joshua built a log cabin there.

In 1730, he combined the log cabin with a larger red-brick farm-house which still stands and is not unlike the one in which I now sit and write out this history. Joshua's property was inherited by his twin grandsons, Joshua and Samuel, at a time when botanical study and exploration, particularly by Quakers, thrived. Joshua and Samuel were not explorers like their Philadelphia neighbor and fellow Quaker William Bartram, but they were lovers of botany and collectors of trees. In 1789, they began to plant some of their property as an arboretum, a scientific-sounding term that means simply a garden devoted to trees. By 1830, Joshua and Samuel tended one of the finest collections of trees in the country.[3]

I first walked in this garden devoted to trees a few weeks after our move to Maplehurst, and less than two days before the birth of the baby girl we named Elsa Spring. Today, this eighteenth-century arboretum is called Longwood Gardens, and it encompasses the Peirce family's original 402 acres, plus an additional 600 acres or so. The day of our first visit was a Sunday, but I had been so weighed down by the burden of impending labor and our stacks of still unpacked boxes that we decided to skip church and take ourselves and our three kids to the botanical gardens we had been told were a must-see.

We walked for hours that day beneath innumerable trees, alongside ponds and classical water gardens, without ever realizing that we'd explored less than half of the place. We would visit again at Christmas with Elsa in a carrier beneath my winter coat and discover the enormous glass conservatory, the waterfall and bell tower, and the extensive show fountains. The land that comprises Longwood Gardens has changed almost beyond reckoning since Joshua Peirce felled the straightest trees he could find and built his cabin. The man largely responsible for those changes was Pierre S. du Pont, the wealthy scion of the Delaware du Pont family and head of the chemical company that bore their name. In 1906, he rode in as if on a white horse and saved every one of the Peirce family trees from the clear-cutting saws of a local lumber company.[4]

On a recent visit to Longwood, my father and I studied the informational placards in the former pump room of Pierre du Pont's famed water fountains. His eyes still on the wall, my father began to speak, as if reading, but he was telling me a story: "In 1931, when Pierre du Pont was ordering almost $1 million worth[5] of carved limestone for his gardens from an Italian carver's family workshop, my grandfather, your great-grandfather, was struggling to guide a mule through the dust of his cotton field on a small farm in Comanche County, Texas." My eyes moved to my father's face, and I saw in his profile all the men and women who had stood in bread lines or loaded up their belongings during the Dust Bowl days. The placard told us that du Pont's order kept the storied Italian carving enterprise afloat during those years of global economic depression, but I couldn't help thinking, *What business did he have spending so much money on limestone flowers, vases, and turtles? Was his placemaking a needless extravagance? A let-them-eat-cake obliviousness?*

"Do you think he was wrong to spend that money?" I asked my dad.

"I don't know," he said, after a long pause. "It's a fine line between foolishness and vision."

The 1906 Pierre du Pont is easier for me to admire. That was the year a thirty-six-year-old du Pont heard that the Peirce family's magnificent trees had been sold to a Lancaster lumber company. Du Pont rushed in to buy the land and the lumber contract, managing to save most of the trees, irreplaceable because of their age and size, and setting in motion his own lifetime devotion to these particular trees and this particular land. In 1912, du Pont compiled a 174-page instruction manual for his property manager, in which he wrote, "No tree, dead or alive, is to be removed or trimmed, no matter whether located on the farm or in the woods, unless by special permission of the owner. The preservation and care of trees is considered of first importance, as their injury is irreparable while time or money (or both) will rectify most other mistakes."[6] This same manual includes a line that makes me laugh: "As the general effect of the place is quaint and characteristic of older days, the owner does not care to keep the lawns in as exact good order as is the custom on modern country places." Those are words I might print out on a card. I could give the card to each lawn care company representative who comes knocking on our door, having seen an entrepreneurial opportunity in our somewhat weedy five acres.

The Mr. du Pont who saved the trees is my hero. The Mr. du Pont who spared no expense on a grand garden vision is a man with whom I sympathize but also worry I might become. One of the first things du Pont did after taking ownership of Longwood, even before modernizing the long-neglected red brick house, was to create a formal flower garden with four paths radiating from a central, round bed with a fountain. He filled the beds with traditional flower garden favorites such as roses, irises, and lilies. His "flower walk" still exists at Longwood, and today, with the help of an enormous and dedicated army of volunteers and full-time employees, it is a constantly shifting palette of seasonal flowers. I've stolen quite a few ideas from that particular spot—new spring bulbs to try, such as the English bluebells properly labeled *Hyacinthoides non-scripta* and tulips with lacy edges like the dark ones named for Vincent van Gogh, and the best method for staking dahlias (rebar stakes and masses of heavy-duty twine). If, as my father said, there is a fine line between foolishness and vision, I fear my love for the beauty of growing things has crowded out everything but the vision. Perhaps visionaries are always, to a certain extent, fools. But what kind of world would this be without them?

Two years after our move to Chicago, when Jonathan and I began to devote more and more of our attention to my empty womb, we requested and were given a two-bedroom apartment at the Windermere. We couldn't make a baby come, but we could prepare a place for one, the way a gardener clears weeds and mulches the soil for a garden that is still only a dream. Friends helped us carry our furniture and belongings from the third floor to a corner apartment on the sixth floor. The round oak pedestal table we had brought with us from Texas had now patiently endured three moves. It fit perfectly in the corner between windows facing south toward the grand museum façade and east toward the color-shifting waters of the lake. At that sixth-floor height, our lake view was obscured seasonally by the lacy tops of the honey locust trees. It felt as if we had moved into a tree house, and we painted the walls a pale sage green. Jonathan moved his desk into one corner of "the baby's room," but we lived with a half-empty room for what felt like an endless forever. I've checked our photograph albums. I've counted in my head. I am not sure, but I think our forever may have been only two years long. Even so, waiting is endless as long as you wait.

In a community where a two-bedroom apartment was a luxury, the longer our second room remained mostly empty, the more foolish I felt. By our second winter in that two-bedroom tree house, I kept the door to the second bedroom tightly shut whenever we had visitors, unwilling to explain why half the room was furnished only with a small bookshelf and a collection of my favorite childhood picture books. The honey locust trees dropped their leaves again, and there was Lake Michigan: a sullen, gray void on the horizon. Joy, my friend and fellow graduate student, was waiting to be married in the spring, and she felt the emptiness too. When she came over for tea one sleety afternoon, she told me she had started growing green grass on her kitchen windowsill. "You're growing what?" I said.

"Green grass," she said. "I bought a packet of wheatgrass seed at the hardware store on 53rd Street. I planted it in empty yogurt containers. Now that it's sprouted, I stick my nose in it, and I run my fingers over it, and I mow it with scissors once a week."

First my jaw dropped, and then I laughed. What a preposterous, wonderful way to wait. Almost as soon as I could, I walked the three blocks up and six blocks over to the neighborhood hardware store. The shelves of that small store were already overstuffed with bags of salt and de-icer and snow shovels in various colors, materials, and price points. But one of the employees agreed to look in the back for me, and he found it: my own small bag of potting soil, my own little packet of seed.

About the time I had soft green grass just beginning to grow in a formerly empty yogurt container on a formerly empty windowsill, Joy asked if Jonathan and I would like to share a plot with her in a community garden in the spring. "It's only a few blocks from here," she said. "We can split the rental fee and the cost of seeds and seedlings. We can take turns watering and weeding, and then we can share the harvest." Jonathan and I decided we needed to walk those blocks ourselves before we made a decision.

We'd never considered vegetable gardening, though Jonathan remembered eating green beans from his childhood backyard, and I could hardly think of my father without remembering the "relish plate" my mother would add to his dinner, and his only, each night. The plate varied with the season, but in summer it always had homegrown hot peppers and a thick-sliced tomato doused with pepper and salt. But I've never been a fan of spicy food, and I wasn't even sure I liked tomatoes.

The garden, when we found it, didn't look like a garden, but a hand-carved sign dangling from a chain-link fence confirmed that we had, in fact, arrived. The vacant lot within the fence was on the far southeastern corner of the university campus. The tall brick chimneys of a water treatment facility, owned by the university, loomed overhead. Inside the fence, we could see a picnic table, large tubs for collecting rainwater, and a grid-like spread of mounded dirt separated by woodchip paths. It seemed there was no reason to say no. The walk from our apartment on 56th Street wasn't far. Joy and her fiancé had grown gardens before. We would enjoy spending more time with them. Of course, we had no notion then that the walk from apartment to garden would grow longer as my belly grew. We couldn't know that one September Joy would welcome us home from the hospital's maternity ward with a dish of pasta studded with cherry tomatoes so sweet, I would finally say with confidence, "Yes, I love tomatoes." But that winter, before anything grew, we did not know how vital empty places can be.

An empty bedroom. An empty garden. This empty patch of lawn. Empty may be in the eye of the beholder, but a visionary placemaker is one who sees something beyond emptiness or fullness. The visionary sees opportunity, like the ghost of a possible future. Pierre du Pont walked with his wife, Alice, in a garden devoted to trees (By all accounts, they were devoted to one another and to their many nieces and nephews, but did they long for babies of their own?), and Pierre's eyes were drawn to the empty spaces between the trees. Thus, with his own hand, he sketched out a formal flower garden, the first of many he would design and plant at Longwood. The "Flower Garden Walk" he planned over the winter of 1906–07 was 600 feet long and centered around a twenty-foot pool with a fountain. Like the garden of my own imagination, it featured four paths radiating out from the center—a long garden with four quadrants. But the element that seems to me the most significant is this: du Pont's first garden was designed with extra-wide paths. Even at this very early stage, du Pont knew he was not creating a garden for himself only, but for family and friends, and—could he have foreseen it?—for the thousands, even millions, who would one day come to see and learn, play and rest at Longwood.

Expansive paths might not seem so meaningful, but they are suggestive of a significant contrast between Pierre du Pont's country home and the country homes of his du Pont forebears and of other American barons of the Gilded Age. The brick house at Longwood is no Biltmore or Newport mansion. It is one of the "brave brick houses" Philadelphia merchant Robert Turner famously praised in a 1685 letter to his governor, William Penn.[7] Pierre du Pont's own Pennsylvania roots do not extend quite so far back. He was the great-grandson of Éleuthère Irénée du Pont, who came to Delaware from France in 1800 and founded a gunpowder manufacturing business that would become the DuPont chemical company. Had the gunpowder business failed,

Éleuthère's backup plan was to open a nursery business. Upon immigrating, he referred to himself in official documents as a "botaniste."[8] It was Éleuthère's great-grandson Pierre who would turn the family business into a corporate behemoth, but he was not the first du Pont to earn a fortune. The Brandywine River Valley is sometimes called "Chateau Country" for the many stately homes and gardens that line the bucolic, brandy-colored creek.[9] One of the most familiar of these is Winterthur, the home of Henry Francis du Pont in Pierre's lifetime, but first constructed by Éleuthère Irénée du Pont's daughter and son-in-law.[10] Today, it is a premier museum of the American decorative arts. Winterthur is a grand estate, but just five miles to the southeast stands one that is more lavish still, the Nemours Estate. This 102-room mansion, built in 1907 by Éleuthère's son, Alfred du Pont, for his wife, was inspired by the Petit Trianon, the Neoclassical chateau at the Palace of Versailles that Marie Antoinette once called home.

Chateaus are not known for their cozy hospitality. They are known for an aristocratic style of entertaining and a pride of place designed to assert and reinforce social hierarchies. But Pierre du Pont's extra-wide walks and, later, his illuminated fountains and the organ he installed in the conservatory are indicative of a kind of placemaking infused with joy rather than pride. Longwood was a source of joy to Pierre, and he simply couldn't contain himself. It gushed in him like one of his own cutting-edge hydraulic fountains. As this company chairman and heir to a fortune would write, "I have set myself and guests to work planting flower seeds whenever I have opportunity."[11] When I am at Longwood, I wonder, *Is there room for others in my vision? Is my vision hospitable? Is my vision born of joy?* When I am at Longwood, I begin to believe that making a place, the way we are meant to make places, is always as much about the giving away and the letting go as it is about the creation process.

We once had very little, and it felt easy, natural even, to push back our tiny sofa and invite everyone to come on in. But we have more now and, paradoxically, I find myself holding it tighter. This isn't selfishness, exactly. It is more like an overdeveloped sense of responsibility. To whom much is given, much is expected, and so it has been harder, with these many children and these many rooms and these many acres, to let myself be reckless. Yet, it is possible that in my caution, I have, brick by brick, walled myself off from joy.

I experienced joy long before I knew a child had finally been given to us. I felt it on a night when the emptiness within me seemed bottomless. One autumn evening, I walked the winding path along Lake Michigan. As I walked, my hopelessness lurched forward into anger, and within myself I screamed at God, *Where are you? Do you even care? Why won't you help me?* I kept my face down, toward my empty womb and my marching feet, but as I rounded a curve in the path I raised my face again with an internal cry, *Where are you?* Then I saw something that stopped me, right then and there, in my tracks. The lake was on fire. I swayed on my feet, disoriented. I did not understand what I was seeing. *It's only the sun,* I reasoned. But this was evening, and I was staring east where no sun could be. Still, there was a ball of fire rising from the water, far out at the horizon yet seeming so near. As if I could touch it. As if I could be burned. As if it might consume me.

It took long seconds, perhaps even a minute, to realize that what I saw was only a full moon. Though it looked like a gargantuan fireball or like some new and menacing planet just come into view, it was the same, familiar moon I had known my whole life. It was, in fact, a phenomenon called "the moon illusion," and it is common enough. Aristotle, writing in the fourth-century BC, described the apparent enormousness of a horizon-hugging moon. Back then, it was thought that the atmosphere had some magnifying property, but now we know that it's all in our heads, though precisely *what* our heads are up to is still a matter of debate. One book on this illusion includes theories by twenty-four different researchers, and no theory emerges a clear winner.[12] We know that the moon does not shift in size, but we do not know precisely why it appears to us to do this very thing. I can't explain the moon illusion, I can't explain why the moon that night felt like an answer, but I can say with confidence that joy and terror are closer to one another than we imagine. Beneath the fiery light of that moon, I felt very small. But I also felt the joy of being seen.

Four months later, on a January night brittle and bright with cold, I stood at the kitchen sink with a positive pregnancy test in my hand, and I cried. These were not tears of joy; they were tears of doubt and confusion. I was alone; Jonathan was out of town for work. Later, he would tell me how, that night, he had walked beneath a full moon on a Florida beach and prayed for a baby. We had endured various fertility tests for a few months now, and I had only taken the pregnancy test to confirm that I could go ahead with an X-ray on Monday morning. I was sure I could not be pregnant, and I hated the hope that sprang up in me at the sight of those two little lines. I was convinced the medicine I'd been taking had altered my hormones and led to this false positive. But then I looked up and out toward the faraway lake. A small triangle of sky was just visible between the Windermere's eastern wing and another tall apartment building near the beach and to the south. That triangle, that sliver, that impossibly small and perfect window of sky was completely filled by a large and brilliant full moon. Then, suddenly flooded with hope, I cried with relief, and I cried for happiness.

Eight months later, we brought our daughter Lillian home from the university hospital. While she slept in a Moses basket on the floor, Jonathan and I sat at the round oak table feeling dazed with exhaustion and exhilaration and dazed as well by the light shining on the water and flickering amongst the shadowy leaves of the honey locust trees. Together for the first time as a family in our tree house apartment, we watched one more full moon rise above the lake.

So there is this empty plot of earth at Maplehurst, and I have had a vision of its fullness, like a moon rising in a black sky. *Do I dare dig in?* Truthfully, if I were alone, the answer might always be *no*. It is good to have a partner or friend when you stand on the precipice of a question like that. "Do I dare?" I ask Jonathan. "Of course!" he answers. And his enthusiasm carries me beyond my doubts and my dithering. Jonathan loves me, and he knows I delight in flowers, and that is enough for him. For now, at least, I will let it be enough for me too. I still wonder if this house of ours, with its old shutter dangling at a crazy angle and its windows too aged and broken to open, has been one colossal mistake. We do not have a du Pont fortune, and I do not know how to ride a horse, white or otherwise, but, as the saying goes, in for a penny, in for a pound. I will say one more *yes*, I will make space within myself for the emptiness of a flower garden, as I once embraced an empty bedroom and an empty plot in a derelict city lot. Why? Perhaps for no better reason than because a full moon rose in the sky on our first night in this house, and for me, the light of it has never completely dimmed. I still see it glimmering in the corners of this place. Teasing me, tempting me, perhaps. But also, I feel sure, urging me on.

A few months after we left Chicago for good, our South Side community garden was bulldozed to make room for a construction staging ground. The university owned that empty lot, and apparently they needed it for diggers and cranes and piles of backfill. But that garden still bears fruit, here at Maplehurst, and at my friend Meredith's Wisconsin house (she and her husband joined us in the garden when Joy moved away), and probably in many other places as well, just as the legacy of Peirce's trees continues, though almost all of those original specimens have died and been replaced. Just as my great-grandmother's long-ago flowers still perfume my father's stories and fuel my own wild dreams of beauty.

A formal flower garden for Maplehurst begins with an empty sheet of graph paper. It begins with an order for a truckload of cheap, local mushroom compost. It begins with a stack of cardboard we've collected in the old red barn. We'll use it to smother the grass and the weeds. But first? We'll call someone with the right machine to dig out the remains of those two old maple trees. We'll make a clean slate, a fresh start, and it will stink to high heaven, and all winter long everyone who arrives at our front door will ask, "What's that big brown pile out there? What are you doing?" and I will try to believe my own words when I answer, "We are making a garden. We are making a place for flowers. Only wait and see what will grow in the emptiness."

Chapter 6

Old-Growth Forest

How to Be a Neighbor

Like many very old trees, the Penn Oak that anchors the edge of the golf course is a study in arrested movement. With its twisted trunk and curling limbs raised toward the sky, it appears to be frozen in the middle of some whirling dance. My older children, Lillian and Thaddeus, insist it looks like Harry Potter's "Whomping Willow." I sometimes imagine that if I stand very still and look at it only from the corner of my eye, I will catch it continuing its dance though no wind blows. Of course, all trees *are* moving—dancing and growing—just as they seem to be. It is only that they are moving at a pace set more by eternity than the rat-race pace at which we typically move and breathe and scurry at their feet. Their histories are wide and deep, and we are witnesses only to a sliver of that breadth. If placemaking is to be a holy endeavor, I think it must operate on the longest timeline imaginable, and trees help us grasp this expanse of time. This doesn't mean old age always outdoes youth. But placemaking with an eternal perspective acknowledges the long-lived experience of a tree as well as the here-today-gone-tomorrow significance of the daylily. Creation is dancing. How will we respond? Do we join in? Do we interrupt or corrupt the dance? Or, perhaps worst of all, do we ignore it entirely?

Creation is dancing. How will we respond? Do we join in? Do we interrupt or corrupt the dance? Or, perhaps worst of all, do we ignore it entirely?

I wish those who built the golf course behind my house hadn't designed it to include the old white oak at all. I wish they had fenced off the tree and established a protective radius against earth-compacting bulldozers and fertilizer runoff. And yes, I wish this beautiful old tree could live forever, like a *tree of life* in my own neighborhood. But I also understand why those golf course builders couldn't do it. Who wouldn't want to use such a magnificent tree to enhance their place? Who wouldn't want to claim it, showcase it, and stamp it on their logo? *Lead me not into temptation, Lord, because, if given the chance to take ownership of beauty, I'm sure I'd do no better.* This tree, though it wasn't felled, has certainly had its life cut short. The magical Whomping Willow of J. K. Rowling's book could at least defend itself.

Humanity's adversarial relationship with the trees is an old story, often told. Humanity has been clear-cutting forests since the Bronze Age. The bare hills of Iceland and Ireland alike were once covered in forests. It was in part a lack of trees—wood needed for shipbuilding and cooking fires—that sent Elizabethan explorers hurtling toward New World shores. Thankfully, not all American forests were sacrificed, but enough were felled to make survivors like the oak that spreads its leafy crown above the golf course that much more special. Sometimes, placemakers make new. Build fresh. Start from scratch. But most of the time, they repair. They restore. They protect. Sometimes, placemaking is nothing more than the refusal to *unmake.*

Sometimes, place-making is nothing more than the refusal to unmake.

Secured to our refrigerator with a magnet is a promotional postcard for a window restoration business. It has been there for months, ever since it landed, unannounced, in the mailbox here at Maplehurst. The image on the postcard shows a quintessential Pennsylvania colonial farmhouse: stout fieldstone walls, multi-paned windows that ripple with wavy glass, and wooden trim painted the traditional burgundy color I see so frequently in old stone houses nearby. "Proudly serving the Brandywine River Valley and beyond!" the postcard says. When I first set aside the pile of familiar junk mail and studied it, I knew that here was what Maplehurst needed: a restoration business local to our county and specializing in the care of original wooden windows. I also knew that this meticulous and expert care was precisely what we could never afford.

When Jonathan and I first visited Maplehurst during a whirlwind two-day house-hunting trip, we encountered a house that had been vastly improved by its previous owners—they dug a new well, updated the old knob-and-tube wiring, and installed a beautiful new kitchen—but extensive repairs, particularly on the home's exterior, were still sorely needed. Still, the windows were the only thing I did not think I could live with. The house did not have air conditioning, but we visited on a rare 100-degree day, and I was surprised at how much heat these thick brick walls could keep out. I know now that those same brick walls were in desperate need of re-pointing, also referred to as tuck-pointing, and the old limestone mortar was fast crumbling away, but I did not understand the importance of that work and saw only the faded red of beautiful old brick. Yet even then, I knew the windows had obviously seen better days, and I assumed we would tear them all out and replace them with something state of the art and covered in sticker accolades for energy efficiency. In fact, while Jonathan and I waited to hear whether our offer on the house would be accepted, we visited the local big box home improvement store and wandered the window aisle, taking notes. We hadn't yet counted the windows, but the price of vinyl replacements was daunting. We might still have begun ordering up new windows as soon as the papers were signed if it hadn't been for our home inspector. He told us the windows were in pretty good shape for their age and recommended keeping them. I wasn't sure what he saw in those windows that I did not, but with a baby due any day and what felt like a thousand boxes to unpack, we gladly pushed the windows to the low end of our ever-growing list of house projects.

I've learned quite a bit about windows since those first days at Maplehurst. If our windows functioned beautifully, I would not have given them much thought, but broken things occupy a great deal of attention when you live with them intimately. I know more about glass, too, perhaps because so many of our old panes are cracked. I know that it is thanks to improved glass blowing processes that we now take smooth, crystal clear glass for granted, but I also know there is beauty in imperfection. The wavy panes of glass that remain in our windows now look to me like miraculous survivors. How is it that something so fragile has endured for so many years? The old glass reminds me that the distortions and imperfections inevitable in human creation don't always detract from beauty. Sometimes they enhance it. They might even be intentional and part of a beautiful design. But like too many modern consumer products, vinyl windows are made to be used, abused, and eventually replaced. They are, every one of them, destined for landfills because they cannot be repaired. If one part breaks, the whole window is useless. If we had replaced our windows as we'd intended, we would have locked ourselves into a replacement cycle that would repeat itself every ten to twenty years. But old wooden windows were made to be cared for because they were made to be repairable. They are vulnerable to decay, but they embrace restoration.

Maplehurst has thirty-nine windows. Five of these are fairly new vinyl windows installed when the previous owners enclosed a small back porch in order to expand and update the kitchen. That leaves thirty-four original wooden windows, complete with broken sash-cords, cracked glass, rotting sills, and, here and there, old wavy glass that sets the world spinning in kaleidoscope colors. Our thirty-four original wooden windows are covered by thirty-four decrepit storm windows. First installed in the 1950s for added weatherproofing, these "storms," as we call them, are decades past usefulness. The aluminum frames are bent, many of the glass panes intended to function like the double glazing on newer windows are missing, and the screens are jagged with holes. The screen covering one of the three windows that together make a large bay window in our bedroom has been colonized by ivy and now seems willing—even eager—to welcome bugs.

This three-part bay window is ideally situated to overlook my dreamed-of flower garden, but for now, the only garden is the one clinging to the window. If I stand in the driveway on the western side of the house and look up, a green ivy curtain billows gently across the second floor, but the view from inside makes my skin crawl. The fleshy white roots of the ivy vines resemble the wriggling legs of a centipede gripping the torn mesh of the screen. I keep that window permanently shut, preferring at least one pane of glass between me and those repulsive roots (though the irony of a gardener who despises the ugly reality of roots is not lost on me). In fact, only some of our windows consent to being opened, and those that do must then be propped up with sticks or, my preferred method, stacks of old books. The rope-like cords that once lifted heavy weights within the window's frame to keep the sash up or down have all snapped, and their frayed ends dangle. Perhaps most dispiriting, the elegant top curve on each of the original windows was covered and squared off with a strip of wood in order to make those flat-topped storm windows fit. The curve of the windows is still visible from inside the house, but, for sixty years or so, no one has seen that once elegant curve from the outside. I am embarrassed to admit that I had never noticed this until I welcomed to Maplehurst the man who sent us that promotional postcard, and he pointed it out to me.

It was the windows that first attracted us to an apartment for sale on Chicago's 48th Street. Unlike so many of the apartments we had looked at previously, these windows were new, vinyl, and energy efficient. Best of all, they could be opened from the top, which meant we could catch lake breezes in this third-floor apartment without exposing baby Lillian to the risk of a fall. The windows meant even more to us after our first winter in our new Chicago apartment home. Visiting neighbors who did not have new windows, we realized how much warmer our apartment was than theirs, and we gave thanks for modern glass coatings and weatherproof seals and for the foresight of the previous owner, who had ripped out the old and installed the new.

When Lillian was six months old, we still lived in our two-bedroom tree house in the Windermere, but it was becoming more difficult for Jonathan to share his home office with a baby, especially since, to our initial surprise, our much-desired miracle child did not have the "angel baby" temperament described in one of our parenting books. At the same time, our friends began buying apartments. First one couple, then another, then a single guy we knew from church. Later, we would look back at these years and see a so-called "housing bubble" growing larger and larger and larger, but Jonathan and I knew only that loans for first-time home buyers were easier than ever to procure, and if our friends could purchase three-bedroom apartments, why couldn't we? We were seven years into marriage, we were parents now, and we had never owned our own home. I was still earning only a small graduate student stipend, but Jonathan had an income we felt we could count on. Surely the only item left for us on the checklist to adulthood was home ownership. Besides, I had always wanted to paint my home without asking a landlord's permission, and Jonathan had always wanted a reason to own his own power tools. If we made a conscious choice to leap from renting to owning, it felt as conscious as dipping our toes in a river and finding ourselves quickly swept away.

Eaton Place on 48th Street was a traditional Chicago six-flat.

Built in 1901 with golden yellow bricks above a base of gray limestone blocks, it had wide stone steps and a gracious glass front door with three apartments on either side. Each apartment was stacked directly on top of the one below, so that every apartment ran in a straight line, like a railroad, from the front of the building to the back. In the front of our third-floor, east-side unit was a large parlor with two windows set into a curve and overlooking the leafy street. A hallway connected the parlor with an enormous dining room. If we think of the kitchen as the heart of the home, I suspect the Victorians thought the same of their dining rooms. The apartment's back door opened out onto a small wooden porch. From the porch you could follow wooden steps all the way down to a scrap of shared yard enclosed by a chain link fence. A narrow alley separated our building from the apartment building next door. The porch faced due north and framed a view of Chicago's famous skyline five miles away. To the right, a sliver of gray lake water was just visible. Every July for years, we sat on our porch with friends and watched fireworks erupt over the lake.

We chose Eaton Place because it was far enough from campus to give us more square footage for a little less money, but it was still close enough for me to walk to my study carrel in the library. I think we also chose it because it straddled a line between old and new, though we never gave that line much thought until moving to Maplehurst. The windows at Eaton Place were new and easy to use, but the ceilings soared in late-Victorian style, and the small hallway between dining room and kitchen was a little like an old-fashioned butler's pantry, fitted out with built-in, glass-fronted cabinets and drawers with filigree handles made of brass. The wooden floors were original and beautifully restored, though you could still see the marks of tiny nail holes where wall-to-wall carpet, a luxury in the 1970s and '80s, had been pulled up and discarded. The main bathroom had once been the victim of an unfortunate fish-themed remodel, but we had always assumed that any city apartment we could afford would need some work. In some communities, new is often more affordable, but in an old neighborhood in an old city, new or newly restored is always more expensive than old. Fortunately, the original kitchen had been remade with much more success than the bathroom. It was "move-in ready," to use our realtor's words. Altogether, the new elements at Eaton Place were convenient, and the old elements were, for the most part, aesthetically pleasing. It is only the wisdom of hindsight that causes me to question these categories. Are old things only worthy of our affection if they don't inconvenience us? Does the new have anything going for it other than ease of use? These were questions I did not think to ask.

Only once in those days did I doubt our commitment to new and improved. One evening, wandering in the dark basement toward the storage closet allotted for our apartment, I stubbed my toe on a stack of wood propped in a cobwebby corner. Peering closer, I realized the stack of wood was a stack of windows. Though only the previous owner of our own apartment had opted to replace all of her windows, every owner had been required to replace their front windows facing the street. The reason, I suppose, was for the visual uniformity of the building. Here, then, were the windows that had been taken out. They had not been thrown away, and, instantly, I could see why: they were one-of-a-kind. The frames were peeling paint, and the hardware was covered in rust or grime—I couldn't quite tell which—but the glass was unlike anything I'd seen before: it was curved, outward, like a bow.

I am not sure, but I imagine that those sashes of curved glass, set two together to make an elegant arc in each parlor, would have embraced the bright light and the warm sunshine in a way that might make all the difference on a gloomy midwinter day. But they had deteriorated and been replaced with the ordinary flat glass windows I so appreciated. I could not then imagine that there had been any other option. Nevertheless, I felt a small weight of sadness settle on my shoulders. I sensed dimly that something wonderful had been lost, and I was disappointed to realize that renovation required such sacrifices.

I do not need to go back to Chicago, back to the basement of Eaton Place, in order to say with confidence what kind of wood was in the curved-glass window sashes stacked beneath the dust and cobwebs. True, I don't know if it was pine, oak, or fir, or perhaps some other species of tree, but I have little doubt it came from a forest we now call virgin, old-growth, primary, or primeval. I imagine this goes without saying, but you cannot find such wood on the shelf of your local lumber store. When the Penns and Bartrams and Peirces first came to the place they called the New World, the land was "an ocean of woods."[1] These were virgin forests that had grown up naturally and been left largely undisturbed by humans. The trees within them, like our still-twirling white oak, had grown slowly beneath their elders in dim and dappled light. As a result, the growth rings in these trees are packed tightly together, and this slow-growth wood is far stronger, more stable, and more resistant to rot and insects than the wood farmed by the lumber industry today. We may still grow the same oak and pine species, yet the word *extinct* comes to my mind. North American old-growth forests are largely extinct, and the wood in every old window at Eaton Place and at Maplehurst is akin to a taxidermy specimen in a museum, one of our few remaining links with vanished places and with trees that can no longer be bought at any price.

When I walk the neighborhood hiking trail that skirts the golf course and the old oak tree just beyond the split rail fence at Maplehurst, I am flooded with nostalgia for the forest that once grew on this spot. But I am hardly the first to register this longing. At the end of that quintessentially American novel *The Great Gatsby*, F. Scott Fitzgerald's narrator, Nick Carraway, reflects on Gatsby's "huge incoherent failure of a house."[2] Gradually, as the "inessential houses" of Gatsby and Daisy's Long Island milieu fade into darkness, Carraway imagines the land as it once was at a significant crux in time:

> I became aware of the old island here that flowered once for Dutch sailors' eyes—a fresh, green breast of the new world. Its vanished trees, the trees that had made way for Gatsby's house, had once pandered in whispers to the last and greatest of all human dreams; for a transitory enchanted moment man must have held his breath in the presence of this continent, compelled into an aesthetic contemplation he neither understood nor desired, face to face for the last time in history with something commensurate to his capacity for wonder.[3]

Like Carraway, I may grieve the loss of "vanished trees," but lumber from primeval woods frames the house that shelters my family. I sometimes think that placemaking is almost unbearably

complicated. Every decision is fraught with unintended conse-
quences. We busy ourselves making new worlds with little

thought for the old we are destroying.
Or, we try to reclaim a lost Eden, but
the new worlds we make often seem
even farther away from that elusive
place. Almost a century after Fitzgerald
wrote those words for Nick Carraway,
I wonder if he was right. When we felled
the trees, did we lose forever those places
capable of touching the very depths of
our God-given capacity for wonder?[4]
Or can we remake such places today?

*When we felled the
trees, did we lose
forever those places
capable of touching
the very depths of
our God-given
capacity for wonder?
Or can we remake
such places today?*

As I tally up the changes we made to Eaton Place, I recall how
often some visitor stepped through our front door and said, "Oh,
my. What a peaceful home." We heard those words or ones like
them so often that Jonathan and I began to ask ourselves why.
Was it only the contrast between our freshly painted walls and
the communal stairwell where old, tattered wallpaper needed
desperately to be replaced? Or had we achieved something intangible with our power tools and paint brushes, our dreams and
our desires? We knew that Eaton Place, Apartment 3 had not
been a peaceful place before our arrival. Our downstairs neighbors told us stories of shouting and broken dishes. The day we
moved in, I found a torn wedding photo on top of a cupboard, and
Jonathan discovered a hypodermic needle under one of the radiators. Those disturbing glimpses of the past only heightened the
anxiety that had been planted in us by a phone call we received

the night before our mortgage closing. The caller said he was the former husband of the young woman selling us the apartment. He thought we should know that the building had a problem with rats. He thought we should know that one of the residents was mentally ill. She never paid the monthly assessments she owed the community, and her hoarding was a fire risk. He didn't want to sabotage the sale. He wasn't on the deed and had nothing to lose or gain. But he thought we should know.

It was fairly easy for me to discount this stranger's words, though I wished he hadn't mentioned rats. I have always had a phobia of rodents, and who could say what horrors lurked in that dim basement I had only briefly glimpsed during our home inspection? Still, it seemed obvious to me he wanted to hurt his ex-wife by convincing us to back out of the sale. But this was our first experience buying a home, and we were rattled. Jonathan, especially, was filled with doubt and fear, and this surprised me. To say my husband is an optimist is to render prosaic a quality that, in him, is pure poetry: he is calm waters, he is sunny skies, he is a glass full to overflowing. *If he's afraid*, I worried, *maybe I should be too.*

Now, having walked with him through a few more last-minute, home-buying nightmare scenarios, I understand how fear pulls the strings of our hearts in different ways. For me, in these years, I feared the emptiness within. I worried that I would go on forever wanting children who would never be born to me. But Jonathan always faced that possibility with trust and faith. For him, fear played on the emptiness without. More than anything else, he worried he might guide his family toward shelter only to find no welcome, as if he were Joseph caught in Bethlehem and the inn was forever full. He knew nothing was stopping us from buying Eaton Place, but he worried that signing our names on the dotted line might turn out to be a horrible mistake.

In legal terms, Eaton Place was organized as a condominium association. We owned the walls of our home and everything within them, but we owned only a percentage stake in the building's communal elements, such as the central stairwell, the boiler, and the flat roof that gave our Chicago building the look of a small English castle. We never saw a single rat, but making decisions with six neighbors about whether and when to repair the building's stonework and at what temperature to set the boiler that heated our radiators was always complicated, never easy or natural. We loved our neighbors, but they exasperated us, as I'm sure we exasperated them. Our downstairs neighbors in particular began by praising us for our quiet (We never screamed! We never smashed dishes!). However, as our family grew (oh, how slowly, how painfully it grew), and those babies stopped crawling and began to run, hurtling themselves down the length of the long hallways, we received frequent phone calls about headaches and other illnesses and the desire for an afternoon nap in peace and quiet. I came to dread the ringing of the phone.

Placemaking is a kind of peacemaking.

Placemaking is a kind of peacemaking. It is a way of making peace within families, for instance when we rearrange the bedroom furniture to better suit siblings who share a room, or when we hang light-blocking curtains in the baby's nursery; it is a way of making peace within communities, when we share our places through hospitality, or when communities of very different people care for a shared space such as a park or garden. Our placemaking at Eaton Place was as much about patience and kindness and careful communication as it was about tile and paint. I sometimes think of it as our own "Holy Experiment," to use William Penn's phrase for his utopian Pennsylvania dream.

We had never owned our own home before, never done any serious remodeling, and though we had lived for years in an apartment community, we had never participated in communal decisions regarding the minimum temperature for winter comfort or whether to replace the peeling wallpaper in the stairwell with new wallpaper or paint. Even an apparently simple question—wallpaper or paint?—involves working through a community's concerns regarding style, budget, maintenance, and quality. The question cannot be answered or acted upon without a shared vision for the place being made. When I purchased new carriage-style ceiling lights for the building's stairwell to replace the 1970s globe lights that had been there previously, I was acting on the responsibility given me by my neighbors, but I was a nervous wreck until I knew they approved of my choice. Yet this experience in sharing ownership of the building that sheltered each one of us taught Jonathan and me so much about the complexities and the beauties not only of making a place but of being a neighbor. No wonder that, since Eaton Place, we have always thought of the word neighbor as a verb.

Jonathan's parents came from Texas to Chicago and helped us remodel our bathroom at Eaton Place. Jonathan's father strapped on kneepads and taught Jonathan how to lay tile as he had once taught him how to shingle the roof on their family's Corpus Christi ranch house. I panicked when they first took a sledge-hammer to the fish-themed tiles, imagining they might somehow bring down the whole building. Jonathan's mother helped me bathe two-year-old Lillian in the kitchen sink. I no longer remember our conversation, but I feel sure I did not tell her how much we wanted to give our daughter a sibling and how, once more, a baby seemed impossible. We could tear down walls, rip up floors, make this home new, but we could not make the family of our dreams.

The finished bathroom was lovely, and I've never had such a pretty bathroom since. Subway tile in creamy white linked the old enameled tub with a porcelain sink on porcelain legs. I found the sink on eBay, and it sat for months on our living room floor, patiently awaiting installation. The floor was finished with old-fashioned, black-and-white checkered tiles. The style was Victorian, but we had found them on the shelf at a local big box store. I hung an etched glass mirror (also from eBay), and Jonathan installed a bright and shiny chrome faucet with an elegant arched neck and handles marked "H" for hot and "C" for cold. I've often wondered how Jonathan's first attempt at tiling has held up. One day, when someone replaces the subway tile, perhaps they will find Jonathan's wedding ring behind the wall. It disappeared sometime during the renovation, and Jonathan has always said it must be sitting on the wooden frame between the walls at Eaton Place.

Our friend Laura was a frequent guest in our spare room at Eaton Place (though that room was only "spare" because it had a bed as well as Jonathan's desk, and Jonathan was always willing to work from the dining room table). I asked her recently if she remembered the fish-patterned bathroom tiles, but she didn't remember them, and she didn't even remember the porcelain sink with its porcelain legs. "What *do* you remember?" I asked her.

"I remember how you would light a candle on the table when the sun went down. I remember a basket of cloth napkins on the counter ready for anyone to grab and use. I remember how you or Jonathan would sprinkle cinnamon in the bottom of the coffee pot in the morning. While the coffee dripped, the whole kitchen smelled dark and sweet. Oh! And I remember that you never even set a jug of maple syrup on the table without decanting it into a glass jar first."

"Maple syrup?" I said, surprised. "But that was only so we could safely warm it up in the microwave."

"Well. It was a very pretty glass jar. And I've never forgotten it."

We were practicing, Jonathan and I, honing our place-making skills through big bathroom renovations and the little cozy touches our friend Laura remembers. Eaton Place was our messy rough draft. No doubt we made some foolish choices as we went around improving our new Chicago home. But Eaton Place was much more than a "practice" place or a "starter" home. Placemaking can transform us as much as it can transform a house. This is true even if, by choice or necessity, we stay in one home for a lifetime. Jonathan and I poured ourselves into that apartment, changing it and being changed in return. We planned a bathroom remodel and became partners working toward a common vision. I tended petunias and impatiens in pots on the back porch and became a gardener. Jonathan built shelves for Lillian's toys and became a carpenter. We became more of ourselves at Eaton Place. I haven't stepped on those varnished wood floors in eight years, but I lived with such focused desire in that home, I still find myself there in my dreams, chasing toddlers down the long hallway between the parlor and the dining room.

The Psalmist says, "Take delight in the LORD, and he will give you the desires of your heart."[5] This promise comes almost immediately after a charge to "dwell in the land." Before Eaton Place I would not have understood this alignment of place and desire, but now I understand that not only do our desires shape a place, places influence what it is we want and what it is we love. Almost immediately after moving into Eaton Place, I painted the great big formal dining room the color of a dried and faded rose because pink has always been my favorite color. Unfortunately, the dusty rose shade didn't work well in that room, where only a little light seeped between our big window and the apartment building two feet away. Some colors need a wash of bright sunshine in order to look their best. Three years later, I finally admitted that I had made a mistake and I couldn't will that color to look any different than it did, no matter how much I loved it. Spreading a fan of paint chips in front of my eyes, I considered not what color *I* wanted, but what color this dark dining room *needed*.

Placemaking is highly personal, but it fails to the extent that it is selfish. I wanted pink, but I could not make that color right. Three years after moving in, I chose new paint colors for the dining room: robin's egg blue for the ceiling, and for the walls, a bright shade of beige called fawn. Jonathan pulled out his beloved power tools while I stirred cans of paint. Together, we added wooden trim about twelve inches beneath the tall ceilings. Then we washed the ceiling and the space above the new molding bright as a painted sky. I tried to keep Lillian and her new baby brother, Thaddeus, corralled beneath the drop-cloth covered table. "It's a tent!" I said with forced glee. Eventually I gave up and painted as best as I could with Thaddeus in the carrier on my back. That night, we ate dinner at our long, black dining table. I sat at one end with Thaddeus in a highchair near my elbow. Jonathan sat at the other, with Lillian on a booster seat between us. The ceiling no longer felt like a ceiling; it felt more like open sky, and Jonathan and I smiled at one another across the table.

I wanted a baby without the agony of waiting and uncertainty, but all these years later I can say with confidence: for me, the harder way was the better way. Remembering how we sat beneath that painted plaster sky, I understand how good it is that the best gifts in life don't simply drop from above. Rarely, if ever, do we pray a simple prayer then watch as the desire of our hearts falls neatly into our hands. Instead, the best gifts, like the gifts of my sons and my daughters, and like the gift of every one of our homes, are those that invite our participation, our prayer, our desire, and only then, when we have so much more to give, our gratitude. Because "a longing fulfilled is a tree of life."[6]

Though I love pretty things and special touches (small as the honey scent of a beeswax candle, large as the curvy porcelain legs of a porcelain sink), like the rest of the world, I have tended to view such things as unnecessary extras. They are indulgences. They are not strictly necessary and should be doled out with caution, like special treats. Surely only an incurable romantic would choose old wooden windows over modern vinyl. But what if beauty is one of the greatest gifts I give my neighbors and my guests? What if my own choices give others the permission they need to forgo the plastic jug, to light the special candle, to sit quietly in the afternoon with milky tea in a bone china cup? I believe beauty reflects the truth about who God is and what this world is all about. What could be more important than cultivating beauty in little ways and large, however I am able?

As you probably realized already, I finally called the number on the postcard from the window guy. We hadn't won the lottery, and I was still full of doubts, but a quiet space opened up one afternoon while the kids ran around outside, and I realized I just needed to *know*. I was compelled as much by the memory of those beautiful old windows in the Eaton Place basement as I was by the disrepair of the windows at Maplehurst. I wanted a window expert to tell me just how bad our windows were and what it might take to repair them. I knew it would be beyond our means, but I also knew it would help me if I could fix that knowledge with numbers, like pins on a bulletin board. Only then could I throw away the postcard. Only then could I make peace with the ivy encroaching on my bedroom window.

I believe beauty reflects the truth about who God is and what this world is all about. What could be more important than cultivating beauty in little ways and large, however I am able?

While the phone rang, I imagined the sound of it bouncing off cubicle walls in some corporate office. I did not know where this window restoration business was headquartered, but I imagined a city like Wilmington, Delaware, or perhaps West Chester, Pennsylvania. Not far from Maplehurst but far enough to be in some place full of beautiful old houses owned by people with the money and the knowledge to properly take care of them. When a man's voice finally answered, I stumbled over my words, "My name is Christie Purifoy. I live in a farmhouse with so many old windows. Can you help me? I'm not sure what to do."

"What did you say your name was?" he asked.

"Christie Purifoy," I said again.

"Hold on, just a minute."

I could hear the rustle of papers. I could hear the phone being picked up again. "Christie Purifoy? I can't believe this." He paused. "I know your house. I drive by it every day. I live quite close to you. My name is John. Last week, I ordered your book

Roots and Sky for my wife. I'm holding it now. This is the house on the cover, isn't it?"

In the space between hearing his words and forming some of my own, I was flooded with relief. I suddenly knew I had been right to pick up the phone and that the timing of my call was also right. For the first time, I felt optimistic that some solution would be found. Maybe we wouldn't fail this house after all. Maybe Maplehurst had not been a mistake. In that small moment, I felt all of these things because the man who answered the phone wasn't only a window restorer.

He was our neighbor.

Chapter 7

Queen Palm

LETTING GO OF A
FORMER HOME

I felt emboldened. I felt hopeful. I had found John—someone who not only respects old wood and old ways of building houses the way Jonathan and I are learning to respect them, but who is also a neighbor and an expert window restorer. The improbability of our encounter had lifted some weight from my shoulders. Or, if the weight remains, it is lighter, for it is shared.

When John came by to inspect our windows and talk about the process and costs of restoration, we discovered our children attend the same nearby school, and we have several friends in common. John told me how, years before, he had exchanged a career in a comfortable office for a career in the restoration business after realizing how much he envied the man who came weekly to mow the lawn outside his office. "I love working with my hands, and I love working outside," he said. John told me our windows were not the worst he had seen. Most were great candidates for repair, but the windows on the third floor concerned him. For some reason, these windows had never been covered by storms and were perhaps only a few years away from becoming unsalvageable. *Unsalvageable.* That word fell like a hammer blow. I still had no idea how we could pay for it, but saving at least the third-floor windows now felt like a moral obligation.

While my husband continues to study bricks and soffits and the rotted wood of the porch, wondering how many repairs he might be able to tackle on his own, I have been feeling out the depths of my sense of duty to this place. I wonder how much of myself, and how much of our financial resources, I am willing to commit toward restoration and salvage. Meanwhile, I have also been scanning local online message boards, searching for helpers. Jonathan's skills in home repair far exceed my own—he even re-pointed the brick wall around our back porch at Eaton Place—but knowing you *can* do a job is a far cry from deciding you *should* do a job. Because I have so few hands-on building skills (my little boys know more about power tools than I do), it has been easier for me to accept that the do-it-all-ourselves placemaking we practiced in our previous homes is never going to be sufficient to meet the needs of Maplehurst. And were we ever really the go-it-alone weekend restorers we've imagined ourselves to be? After all, we didn't renovate that Eaton Place bathroom without help. In so many ways, the needs of Maplehurst are beyond us. On our own we can neither remake this place nor care well for it. Home ownership can be a heavy burden if we carry that burden alone. I am beginning to suspect this is true whether we live in a condominium or a farmhouse. Yet there is another way; there is caretaking pursued in community.

The gaping hole in our wooden roofline molding where that

piece of rotten wood once fell at my feet remains one of the most pressing needs, if only because it is the most obviously decayed portion of the home's exterior. And not only is there a chunk missing, but the paint on all the rest is peeling, flaking, and lined like an alligator's skin. It makes our house look neglected. It makes our house look unloved. I found a carpenter/painter online, and he came out to take a look at Maplehurst. Jonathan was at work, but I walked this local handyman around the perimeter of the house, explaining that we needed the hole in the molding repaired and the rest of the wood stripped and repainted. It seemed like a simple enough task to me. The only complication I could foresee was how anyone would reach the highest portions of the roofline three stories up. But the handyman saw far more than that. He didn't say much, but when we finally stood in the front lawn looking up toward the porch and the front façade of the house, he said quietly, "You can't buy molding like that on the shelf at the lumber store. I wouldn't even know how to begin." And just like that, he punctured the balloon of my hopeful momentum.

I never planted a tree while I lived at Eaton Place. There wasn't room for one. I learned to live according to seasonal rhythms by growing flowers in the two stone urns that flanked our building's entrance. When the seasons shifted, pansies gave way to geraniums, which then gave way to chrysanthemums. I filled window boxes on our back porch with scented petunias, but each September I cleaned them out. The rhythm of the seasons is a rhythm of birth and death and rebirth. Without faith in this larger pattern, so much can feel wasted and without meaning, too ephemeral to matter. Life can seem like little more than a litany of the things we lost in winter. When I take inventory of my Eaton Place memories, I see much that has gone. There was the slouchy green velvet club chair we kept in a corner by the fireplace. We no longer have the chair, and I can't remember where or when we let it go, but I remember crying in that chair after yet another negative pregnancy test. In the same room, there was also an oriental-style rug. The polyester fibers were soft, and I used to kneel there when I begged heaven for just one more baby. That rug, too, has gone. I think we gave it to friends who later lost it in a flood. Of course, the small chandelier I hung in the entryway, the porcelain sink with its porcelain legs, and the butler's pantry with its warm wood and brass hardware have also gone, though I tell myself some other family still enjoys them.

Also lost to me is the playground a block away from Eaton Place where I went almost every day with Lillian. One October afternoon, my dear friend Aimee walked past the park and saw me there, near the swings. She walked over, we hugged, and as I pulled my blue silk cardigan closer around my already exhausted and nauseous body (a cardigan I bought years ago in Ireland and still wear), I whispered that I was pregnant again. Finally. Pregnant. And eight months later, there on the front steps of our building, I sat down suddenly near the urns filled with red geraniums because the baby was coming, too fast. My downstairs neighbor patted my arm, saying, "Oh, honey," and Jonathan waved me toward the open door of our car. Thaddeus was born fifteen minutes later at the hospital nine blocks away. It was my birthday.

Lillian, now twelve, has grown to nearly my own height, and she recently wore my blue silk cardigan to a wedding. Baby Thaddeus is now only a memory, having been replaced by a fourth-grader with freckles on his nose, but he and I still celebrate new life together every twenty-third of June. I still tend geraniums. Eaton Place exists only in our memories, though there is still an apartment building in Chicago I could visit again if I wanted. But I am not sure I want to go back. Somehow, return does not seem possible. Or advisable.

My friend Aimee once glimpsed the inside of Apartment 3 while visiting our friend Tracy, who moved into Eaton Place with her family not long before we moved out. "It isn't the same at all," Aimee said. Which means more, I think, than that the green velvet chair and the polyester rug are no longer there. Also no longer there is the four-poster bed in the room with champagne-colored walls where our second son, our third child, was born on the first warm day in spring. We had waited for him too, but with more hope and less grief, and because we had chosen a nurse-midwife who would come to us for the birth, his arrival was less dramatic if no less intense. Every year on his April birthday, Beau asks me what time he was born, but without the ceremony of those official hospital protocols, the precise time, if it was recorded, has never been cemented in my mind. All I remember is that he was born just as the sun began to illuminate the cherry blossoms brushing against our bedroom window. "It was early morning," I tell him each year. "You came to me with the first flowers of spring."

We didn't leave Chicago because it grew hard to live there, though it did grow harder to live there as our family grew. After Beau was born, I did the grocery shopping by carrying him in a sling, placing Thaddeus in one seat of our double stroller and filling the other seat with groceries. Lillian followed along on her balance bike. The most difficult part was carrying Beau and the groceries back up three floors to our kitchen. Lillian and Thaddeus sometimes begged to be carried too, and I would leave them, either weeping or screaming, on a step somewhere between the first and third floors. Once, my downstairs neighbor found two-year-old Thaddeus near the street about to run for the park a block away. In spite of the challenges, some of my sweetest memories are those of the placemaking we did out of necessity in the apartment that grew smaller over the years we lived in it. For Beau, we tucked a small dresser into a corner of our bedroom. Shelves above the dresser held his own little baby things—a photo album, a collection of Beatrix Potter picture books, and a basket of swaddling blankets. We borrowed a mini co-sleeper bed from Aimee and her husband Rand, and it fit exactly in the space between our bed and the window. And we mounted cut-glass knobs the color of amber near our front door and about two feet from the ground. Our coat closet had filled up long ago, so Lillian and Thaddeus hung their coats and jackets on fiery, faceted glass.

We shape places by living in them, and so much of our placemaking is unintentional, unplanned, or simply given, like grace.

We shape places by living in them, and so much of our placemaking is unintentional, unplanned, or simply given, like grace. Two sons were given to us during those years in Eaton Place, and while their births shaped the place in obvious ways (we rearranged bedrooms, used covered baskets for under-bed storage, and received ever more unhappy phone calls from the downstairs neighbors), I have lately been asking myself, with urgency, whether the intensity of our living left any kind of lasting mark at all on Eaton Place or the neighborhood of Hyde Park or the city of Chicago. When we pack up our boxes and leave, are we erased from that place? Or does our placemaking leave a more enduring legacy?

One of the last things we did in Chicago was to stand, with our three children, and watch the narrow prairie that lay between Eaton Place and the lakefront burn down to ash. This small city park was a triangle of native prairie grasses tucked between a high-rise apartment building and the zipping cars on Lakeshore Drive. When the grasses and perennial sunflowers grew tall each summer, you could walk the boardwalk trails without seeing one bit of the city around you. Only the sounds of those cars—and especially the distinctive screech of the Chicago Transit Authority buses—told you where you still were. In late winter, around the time we began keeping a daily watch for signs of spring, the Chicago Fire Department would visit the little prairie with blowtorches. Prairies need fires, even in the city; it is the only way fresh new grass can grow. The ash enriches the soil and clears it, making way for new spring growth. On a cold, still day in March, we stood across the street from the prairie park. Firefighters in full suits held their blowtorches to the tall, bleached grass. Other firefighters stood ready with hoses in case the fire grew out of control. Thaddeus and Lillian stood still as stone. Mesmerized. And waiting. Slowly, the flames licked the grass. Smoke drifted toward the lake that sat, still and shining, just on the other side of the busy road, and I felt the smoky burn fill my nostrils. I followed the smoke with my eyes and noticed a daytime moon observing us from a corner of the pale winter sky.

When we pack up our boxes and leave, are we erased from that place? Or does our placemaking leave a more enduring legacy?

Were the wildfires already burning when we first arrived in Florida? Perhaps not. I believe those devastating fires began a few months later, after the heat of summer. That's when our cardboard boxes were finally empty, and we began to look around and really see our new home. But in my memory, it seems as if we followed a pillar of smoke straight from Chicago to northeastern Florida. In March, just before we moved, I wore a funny hat on my head, like a burgundy velvet pillow, and accepted my doctorate in English literature at a ceremony within the gothic extravagance of the university's Rockefeller Chapel. When the job interviews I'd had three months previously came to nothing, Jonathan told his global company he was finally able to accept a new position beyond Chicago. "Wonderful!" his superiors said. "We've been waiting for this. We have a job for you in Florida." When Jonathan told me, I thought about leaving behind the golden honey locust leaves and the fact that Beau would be too young to remember snow, and I cried. Jonathan let me cry, but eventually we cheered ourselves with talk of a garage where we could unload groceries without climbing any stairs and fenced-in green grass where the kids could play without supervision, and we said yes to the next thing, the next step, a new home.

A month before Jonathan was to begin his new job, I received a phone call from a liberal arts college in New England with whom I had interviewed before being turned down for a tenure-track position in their English department. "We've had a candidate decline our invitation for a second interview," the woman on the phone explained. "You're next on our list. Could you give your job talk here on campus?" It was the call I'd been waiting for, but it came too late. We'd said yes to Florida, and that yes felt right, even if it also felt hard and uncertain. Even now, looking back, I can't quite explain why I told that school no. It was a crossroads, as clear as any diverging path in a forest, and I made my choice, choosing, I think, to believe that the timing of the phone call had not been accidental. Choosing also, I feel sure, that the zig and zag of our marriage meant that after almost ten years, it was Jonathan's turn to pursue a new professional opportunity. Because of that phone call, I cannot now say that I did not choose Florida. I cannot say I only drifted there because no other option was given me. I chose it, though I did not know what I was choosing.

What had I chosen? What was waiting to be received in Florida? A suburban ranch-style house stuccoed with pale pink seashells. *Coquina*, the finish was called. An orange tree on one side of the house, and a tangerine tree on the other. A banana tree. And a trio of rustling, regal queen palm trees that seemed to have walked straight out of some Hollywood vision of paradise. Every tree was so astonishing, so unlike anything I had ever associated with home, that I was beguiled. Who knew what delights lay in store for us in this strange and strangely beautiful place? The last few years of city living had worn us down with too many stairs, too little yard, and too many of my days spent shuttered up in the university library. At the goodbye party our church threw for us before we boarded a plane for Florida, my friend Pam told me she felt like this new season in Florida would be a season of rest for us. Listening to the palm trees whisper, I considered her words and realized I believed them.

What I did not yet know is what so many others have learned before me. Rest comes in the barrenness after the fire. Rest comes when we are stripped of our usual consolations and distractions. "The wilderness is a place of rest," insists Christian conservationist David Douglas, but his own sojourns in the literal desert of the American Southwest offered him rest "not in the sense of being motionless, for the lure, after all, is to move, to round the next bend."[1] Instead, he continues, "The rest comes in the isolation from distractions, in the slowing of the daily centrifugal forces that keep us off balance."[2] In this sense, the wilderness is a fruitful place, but the "crops" of wilderness, Douglas explains, are silence and solitude. The wilderness traveler who reaps this twin harvest is more at risk of being found than of becoming lost.

Our family had rounded a bend, and I was intrigued. I wanted to see more. *What's next?* I thought with anticipation. But what was next was exactly like standing by the prairie park and watching it burn seemingly to nothing. In Florida, though we would make the same investments in placemaking we had always made, our efforts would seemingly yield no return. If I had spent time and money painting and repainting the Eaton Place dining room, I knew it was worthwhile because I hosted baby showers in that room and Thanksgiving dinners and one memorable church supper when we brought in extra tables and seated forty (forty!) for pasta and salad. But in Florida? In Florida, despite every effort we made, we would eat two Thanksgiving dinners alone with our three children, I would fail to find anyone else interested in a mother/toddler playgroup, and we would gather no one for the church small group we had offered to host. Our lives would feel like a scorched field until the day I stood on a farmhouse porch observing the ghostly remains of a nineteenth-century orange farm and heard an entirely new dream begin to murmur among the moss-drifted oaks.

At Eaton Place, we were accustomed to passing our neighbors on the stairs. We were used to holding doors for one another, chatting on the front steps. Sometimes, I found myself on the same CTA bus with one of my neighbors, heading back from the class I taught downtown. In Florida, we drove air-conditioned vehicles directly into two-car garages and the automatic door closed silently behind us. Lifting groceries from the trunk of my car and carrying them straight through into our new kitchen was a convenience I relished, but we struggled to meet anyone in our new neighborhood. All summer, we remained sealed off from one another by central air-conditioning, garage doors, fences, and screened-in porches. Comfort became the enemy of community. Eventually, we met the neighbors next door. Belle and Joe were a retired couple from Long Island raising three grandchildren near in ages to our own three kids. They talked about New York the way we talked about Chicago. We commiserated over the lack of good pizza, and we praised the fresh, local shrimp. Perhaps because they shared our astonishment at finding themselves in this semi-tropical landscape, they were the ones who told us we would need to buy a pole saw in order to properly prune our queen palms.

On the day I met Joe, he gave me a tour of their yard. It was a typical quarter-acre suburban plot, just like our own, but he was rightly proud of his perfect St. Augustine grass, the coarse, weed-like plant that serves for lawn in hot climates like Florida and Texas. I remembered the rough stuff well, but not fondly, from my childhood backyard. He warned me that it wasn't possible to keep a St. Augustine lawn alive without irrigation, chemical fertilizers, and pest control. "You'll think it's doing fine, but one day . . . Blam! Blam! All brown!" Next he pointed out the bristly bottlebrush tree near his front window. My tree encyclopedia tells me that the leaves of *Callistemon citrinus* have a lemon odor when bruised, but I missed my opportunity to test this claim.

The plant is technically more of a shrub, but Joe's specimen had been carefully pruned upward and thinned out to four or five smooth trunks. The flowers looked as you would expect given the plant's name, yet still, somehow, entirely surprising; they were red and wiry and looked exactly like the brushes used to clean baby bottles.

I liked the soft, loose way Joe pronounced "bottlebrush" so that it sounded more like *bawdle-brush*. It made me think of northeastern places I had only ever visited at the movies. I liked the way he placed his hand on the lovely, soaring trunk of his own queen palm and patted it, gently. I worried over his lawn comments. I couldn't imagine pouring chemicals on the grass where my children played, nor could I envisage paying for a lawn service. I thought we'd probably take our chances. But I was grateful to know why his palm trees looked so much nicer than ours: regular use of a pole saw. Like the pin oaks I had encountered in northern Virginia, many palm trees hold on to dead, marcescent fronds like a faded skirt beneath their new growth. They'll shed those dead fronds on their own eventually, but conscientious Florida gardeners neaten up the trees with clippers and saws attached to long poles. Feeling the weight of responsibility on our shoulders, Jonathan and I made a visit to the hardware store for a pole saw and a lawn mower. We had wanted space of our own for the children to play, but maintaining that space required specialized knowledge and a commitment to routine care. Failing at any of these maintenance tasks could land us on the naughty list with the "beautification board" of our local homeowners association.

A pruning guide for queen palms advises checking the base of each frond before cutting it away. If the base of the leaf stem is still green, the frond isn't fully dead and should be left alone.

Fronds can droop and dry out but still have some necessary life in them. *Is this life, or is this death?* It should be one of the easiest questions to answer, but I have found it to be one of the most mysterious. Our palms hadn't been trimmed in a long, long while, and each one wore a thick, dusty, marcescent skirt. Cutting away the dried-out fronds was a painstaking task. The kids and I watched Jonathan take his time, selecting, sawing, until one frond at a time caught the air and drifted down to land at our feet. Lillian and Thaddeus danced around, waving fronds above their heads and making a pile of them. If we had lived on one of the farm properties bordering our suburban neighborhood, we would have burned the dead fronds right there. Instead, we gathered them and left them in a teetering stack near the mailbox. Once a week, a truck with two uniformed men came by for "yard waste collection day." Perhaps the wildfires that raged through Florida during our first year there began when someone with a bit of land chose to burn their yard waste. Or perhaps the fires were started by lightning strikes. Certainly, the underlying cause—drought—was a natural one, though it may have been exacerbated in unnatural ways. The queen palms signaled paradise, but our new paradise was parched, dying, and eventually it would burn.

In December, while thousands upon thousands of singular snowflakes fell on Eaton Place, the prairie park, and the gray, churning, ice-edged waters of Lake Michigan, I sat with my three children on a long brown sofa in a pink seashell house. Smoke from the wildfires, like an evil fog, clouded the sliding glass door behind our heads. I leaned over and gave Thaddeus one more puff through the spacer of his little red inhaler before I picked up another picture book. Slowly, with nowhere else to be, we turned page after page, dipping again and again into our stack of Christmas storybooks. The Christmas tree in the corner of the room smelled like the fresh air of a mountain-top forest, but it had traveled hundreds of miles on the back of a flatbed truck before we chose it at the tree lot. By the glow of Christmas lights, I read, *Once upon a time, it was winter. Once upon a time, we watched snow fall. Once upon a time, we breathed clear, cold air until tears hovered on our lashes, and we saw the world as if through bright, faceted gems.*

I loved Chicago and poured some vital part of myself into it, but it could not remain mine. In Florida, I was like a marcescent tree, a pin oak, or a queen palm, holding on to an old way of life, desperate to believe that the things we had lost—the particular beauties of a place and its people—would be replaced with new gifts only Florida could give. Instead, Florida merely burned away the old and gave us little but emptiness in return. Of course, eventually the emptiness would lead us to Maplehurst. However, having lost Chicago and having learned in Florida that such a loss is not easily restored, perhaps I am afraid to love Maplehurst the way I once loved Chicago. Perhaps I am afraid to give myself away again. Is that why I have begun to feel this urge to cut and run? To admit defeat and leave this money pit for someone else to fix? I have begun listening to secret doubts. *Was our farmhouse dream a mistake? Will we fail this place? Will this place ruin us?* Yet I remain stubbornly convinced that, in some larger sense, I have found the only place for me. Having wandered through so many diverse landscapes and climates and communities, I know that I am now most at home tucked within green hills and sparkling streams while four seasons shift like clockwork around me and flow like music overhead. At nearly forty, with four children, and the work of writing and gardening to fill my days, I need this place of unique beauty and singular history.

For better and for worse, my chosen habitat is Penn's Woods, the place where an Old World placemaker planted his vision of utopia and reaped a harvest of disappointment. Though he considered the "Holy Experiment" of Pennsylvania his greatest accomplishment, by the end of his life, Penn predicted with disillusionment that the motivations of the present colonial government were not likely to result in utopia.[3] This home of mine, this place where all my dreams have brought me, is in some ways the bittersweet fruit of a failed experiment in placemaking. That is my inheritance, and I do not yet know what lies beyond my own disappointments. The esteemed American biologist and author Edward O. Wilson writes, "The crucial first step to survival in all organisms is habitat selection. If you get to the right place, everything else is likely to be easier."[4]

> *We often discover "the right place" only through trial and error, wandering and waiting, following and believing. Quite often, the right place is, for a season at least, the place where everything is harder, the place where we feel least at home.*

The complication for humans, however, is that we often discover "the right place" only through trial and error, wandering and waiting, following and believing. And our journeys are spiritual even more than they are ever geographical. Quite often, the right place is, for a season at least, the place where everything is harder, the place where we feel least at home.

Chapter 8

Crape Myrtle and Chestnut

SEARCHING FOR A
NEW HOME

Did we choose Maplehurst, or was it chosen for us? This question appears to be a simple one, but it is as complicated as asking, *Who is responsible for an orchard, the one who plants the trees or the one who creates them?* That God chooses places for his people is a foundational element of the story the Bible tells, but a common mistake we make is to assume that the right thing will be an easy thing. Even the Promised Land was full of intimidating giants. God may choose places for us, but he invites us to participate in the making of them, and this participation requires the kind of faith and courage that can look a great deal like foolishness. Still, I can't help but wonder if Maplehurst was intended for our care. Could we have misled ourselves through some Pinterest-or HGTV-fueled delusion? The answer must lie in Florida, the place where our farmhouse dream began.

Unhappiness makes it difficult to see and understand a place. It is like smoke or fog in that way. Even while I lived there, my view of Florida was veiled by my homesickness for Chicago and by my longing for snow and cherished friends and the wide, inviting top of that warm, covered radiator where I would sit reading in the sunshine that poured in through a bay window. Remembering Florida is like raking my hand through sand in search of beach glass; the memories are all in bits and pieces, but a few of them catch the light and shine. I remember our new home was stuccoed in pearly seashells. It looked white from afar, but close up it was pale pink and luminescent. I remember our new home was surrounded by endless tracts of longleaf pines. They looked like forests of delicate feather dusters. So tall and straight and open were the trunks of these distinctive pine trees, they might have been transplants from the Narnian forests of my imagination. Nearer the ground were the impenetrable sword blades of the native saw palmetto shrub. Every time I caught a glimpse of palmetto, I imagined sixteenth-century Spanish explorers leaving their fort on the coast in St. Augustine and hacking their way through a hostile landscape and felt again the surprise of calling such an inhospitable place *home*. I remember our new home was only a few culs-de-sac and strip malls away from a series of hauntingly beautiful river roads. Along the giant St. Johns River, live oak trees swung mossy draperies in southern gothic splendor.

One tree, planted in nearly every yard in our new neighborhood, should have been familiar to me. *Lagerstroemia*, or crape myrtle, is sometimes called the lilac of the South. Michael Dirr is effusive in his praise of this genus. "To travel the South from

June through August," he writes, "is to understand why crape myrtles are the best flowering shrubs/trees for gardens large and small."[1] A few years ago, I was talking with an old friend when she casually described our shared Texas hometown as the "crape myrtle capital of Texas." I nodded along as if I knew just what she was talking about, but behind my half smile, my mind was frantically sifting. I found no memories of crape myrtles from Bryan, Texas. None. Not one. Before my friend had spoken so casually, so knowingly, I would have sworn I had never seen a crape myrtle tree in brilliant summer bloom until we moved to northeastern Florida. For in addition to the orange, the tangerine, and the banana trees in our yard, we had a scrubby, overgrown crape myrtle with fluffy, hot pink flowers while every one of our neighbors had at least two, and sometimes three or more, lovingly trimmed crape myrtles flowering all summer in long panicles of white, electric pink, and a sticky-sweet red the color of overripe strawberries. Crape myrtles bloom explosively, like fireworks. Yet if I had ever noticed them as a child, I had also managed to forget them. Every place has some gift to give, but this gift was one it seems I had long ago refused.

In Florida, I encountered so many botanical relics of my Texas childhood—St. Augustine grass, crape myrtles, southern live oaks—it seems to me now as if I had taken some long, circular journey. There I was, back at my beginning. Perhaps I needed to reacquaint myself with some of the things Jonathan and I had lost when we chose to flee the South twelve years before, and perhaps I needed to reaffirm that choice. Choices are always powerful. It does not matter that we rarely understand exactly what we are choosing. Perhaps that is precisely where the power lies: not in the choosing but in the learning how best to live with our choice.

Though the beaches were beautiful, the place we most appreciated in Florida was a nearby county park called Alpine Groves, about fifteen miles inland from the coast. Our neighbor Joe was the first to tell me about it. He said he liked to take his grandkids for a cup of Italian gelato at a place in a nearby strip mall and then drive just a few minutes down the William Bartram Scenic and Historic Highway to the park. He didn't tell me much about the park itself, so I was unprepared for the wonder of what we found there: walking trails through deciduous forests, a long dock stretching out into the enormous width of the St. Johns River, and best of all, the ghostly remains of a nineteenth-century orange grove homestead, including a white-painted farmhouse, a citrus sorting shed, and horse stables. Every building was empty but for echoes. Here was a different Florida from the one where we rode bicycles in and out of winding culs-de-sac. That Florida was largely imported from the tropical south coast: queen palms, flowery but thorny bougainvillea vines, and key lime trees served up with a helping of southern staples like St. Augustine grass and crape myrtle. But the Florida of Alpine Groves was older than state boundaries and had more in common with Savannah than Miami. Here were bald eagle nests high up in hardwood hickory trees. Here were live oaks draped in moss and, moving slowly and obdurately on the edge of the landscape, a river wider than

Choices are always powerful. It does not matter that we rarely understand exactly what we are choosing. Perhaps that is precisely where the power lies: not in the choosing but in the learning how best to live with our choice.

any modern highway, where Florida manatees bumped placidly along between saltwater and fresh like cows who had chosen the sea.

I could hardly explain to myself why, but I was drawn as if by some strong current to the front porch of that old white farmhouse. I brought Lillian, Thaddeus, and Beau to Alpine Groves as often as I could. They always wanted to play on the playset and swings in another area of the park, but as soon as they would let me, I led them down the path toward the farmhouse. While they played games on the grass beneath the dipping and swaying live oaks, I sat on the front porch steps and watched the river. Sometimes the kids chased each other round and round the house, stopping only to peer inside the wavy glass of the old, wooden windows. The house was always locked, but through one window we could still see a table and a chair in what must once have been the kitchen. I used to think it looked as if someone had just scraped the chair back, given their mouth one final wipe, and headed out for a day spent sorting oranges into crates. Those crates would have made their way by train to Savannah and then by boat to fruit sellers in Queen Victoria's England.

At Alpine Groves, it was no longer possible to tell where the fruit trees had once grown. Northeastern Florida had a thriving citrus industry in the eighteenth and nineteenth centuries, but a series of severe freezes in the late 1800s killed the trees and drove the industry south, leaving its mark in the northeast only in place names like Fruit Cove and Orange Park, and in these empty buildings, the last nineteenth-century structures in the area. Long before even this farmhouse had been built, William Bartram had been so impressed with the indigo and citrus crops growing along the St. Johns River that he established his own estate nearby, but his endeavor didn't succeed, and all remains of it were quickly erased from the landscape. Perhaps Bartram gave up his dream of growing oranges after the astonishing snowstorm of 1774. Such an event was so unprecedented, so rare, that an 1885 Florida history book claims the storm was long remembered among local residents as the "white rain."[2]

I missed Chicago's white rain, but over those months of bringing my sorrow and my loneliness to the front porch of an empty farmhouse, I did not dream of returning. I did not want to go back. But at the same time, I didn't know what I wanted. I had run out of dreams. My adjunct teaching position at a local university was worse than a disappointment. The English department offices were endless corridors of closed doors, and I felt unseen and unappreciated. I struggled to reconcile the low pay with the cost of Beau's babysitter, especially when most of my students seemed so uninterested in the books we read together. Our new church was full of friendly faces, but the few friends we made all lived on the other side of an enormous, spreading city. Yet the peace of that porch, where generations of farming families had enjoyed the breeze off the river, spoke of other ways of living. It spoke of a fruitful relationship to place that was somehow eluding me in our tangle of dead-end suburban streets. It told me home can have a purpose; it can be so much more than the place where you lay your head between Little League games and swim meets and parent/teacher meetings.

I did not then imagine a farmhouse of our own. I certainly didn't imagine a thoroughly suburban farmhouse like Maplehurst with its ring of quiet streets and many neighbors. Still clinging to hope of an academic career, I could not conceive of a life lived anywhere but in some college town or university city. But the hours I spent on that porch must have prepared me for the image that would shake up every one of my long-held plans.

It was a picture in a magazine, of all things. I still have it, tucked in my old journal. When I pull it out, I see a white-painted farmhouse with orange pumpkins on the porch. It looks a little like the Florida farmhouse, but the maple trees in fiery colors place it somewhere in the north. When I turned the page in that magazine and first saw the picture, I noticed a small, third-floor window and thought, *What a lovely space for a writer. She could work but still watch her children—four, probably—running on the lawn.* Then I began to cry, though I hardly knew why. I could not then have said that the pain in my chest was longing. This photograph was like a window on a life I had never thought to want. But the whole experience was so moving and so mysterious that I cut out the picture with scissors and tucked it in the same journal where I wrote things like, "How long, LORD, how long?"[3] Today, I return that journal to the gap on the bookshelf in my third-floor writing room. I lean toward one of the two small windows, and I can just see my four children chasing chickens on the lawn.

The days are long in the Sunshine State. Lillian, Thaddeus, and Beau had all the time necessary to learn that spring smelled like orange blossom and winter was for picking fruit in the backyard with stepladders. I learned how to sit still on a porch and let the breeze stir up new dreams. The great gift of any spiritual or geographic wilderness is that you lose your habitual sense of purpose. This was Florida's gift to me. It can feel as if you are only existing aimlessly, but this aimlessness frees you to live in the present and, eventually, to dream new dreams. It surprises me now to realize just how rooted in the past our new dreams would be. The farmhouse dream—when it emerged—seemed to us entirely new, yet it grew naturally from my family's farming past and the traces of the past I discovered at Alpine Groves. Perhaps we can discover the next right step by turning our gaze and studying the past as if it is a landscape spread out just behind our backs.

In Florida, I rested. In Florida, I did things because I enjoyed doing them, not because they made sense, either according to the spiritual tenets of hospitality or the cultural tenets of financial responsibility. In Florida, Jonathan learned how to make pizzas on an outdoor grill, and we ate every messy bite ourselves because we had so few friends. In Florida, I painted our master bedroom pale pink—the color of the inside of a seashell—and I decided not to care if it made our house harder to sell one day. In Florida, I gathered my courage and spray-painted the conventional brass chandelier over our kitchen table turquoise, and then I painted a few more things turquoise and feasted my eyes on a color that would never have felt right in Chicago.

In Florida, my garden-loving younger sister Kelli visited with her husband Shawn and their three kids, the same ages as my own. While Shawn took over the grill (with skill and enthusiasm), Kelli went out and bought a vivid pink bougainvillea to grow over my backyard fence. She also told me to toss zinnia seeds in my flowerbeds. The bougainvillea died the following winter after a spell of freezing weather, but I planted scented jasmine with starry white flowers in its place. The zinnias thrived in rainbow colors, and I was astonished to discover that so much beauty could be had for the price of a single seed packet. Jonathan built raised beds in the backyard, and when my vegetable seedlings withered (for lack of sun, or excess of heat?), I filled those beds with herbs instead. In Florida, I loosened my grip on my longtime dream of a practical teaching career, and I began to write, first in that journal with its green cloth cover, then on the internet beneath a photograph my sister Kelli took of me on that Alpine Groves front porch.

In Florida, I bought a tiny wooden rocking chair at a yard sale and painted it a glossy silver-gray. The chair was already too small for Beau (he had grown so much since leaving Chicago), but somehow I didn't care. That freshly painted chair lifted some of my gloom. In Florida, we replaced the shiny 1980s brass knobs on our kitchen cabinets with knobs made of turquoise ceramic and embossed with a pattern of flowers and leaves. They were costly, and I worried they would be liable to chip, but they were so unique that they instantly made our home look cared for and special. I installed matching turquoise knobs on our TV cabinet, and that flimsy piece of furniture suddenly looked like a custom work of art. We made our house and yard pretty because we enjoyed it, and because we almost couldn't help ourselves, not because anyone but us would ever see it. In Florida, I set aside the books I'd intended to read in preparation for writing an academic article on Scottish poetry of the 1930s, and I began checking out library books on chicken keeping and beekeeping and vegetable growing and yogurt making and bread baking and memoir writing, and I quit my job at the university. *It's only temporary*, I told myself. "I'm just taking off one semester," I told the program coordinator.

In Florida, we moved Beau into a little white toddler bed and packed up our baby crib for good, but when one month I thought—with astonishment—I might be pregnant again, we realized that maybe there was something better than our old plans. Our hearts said maybe. Then our hearts said yes. I wasn't pregnant, but a door in our hearts had been opened. Desire grew over many months, painfully, as desire always grows until, with no help from a doctor or a prescription, I became pregnant one more time and knew, almost from the first moment, that this baby would be the sister Lillian had long been praying for. But with our growing baby girl came asthma, a relic of my childhood I thought I had outgrown. My doctor couldn't tell me what was causing it. Maybe it was hormones, he said. Maybe it was the tree pollen that was coating our world in yellow dust because the winter weather had turned unusually warm. And he could offer little assurance that the asthma medicines I was now forced to take would be safe for an unborn baby.

A whole new life, one we would never have dreamed of on our own, was quite literally growing within me, but I was immobilized. For weeks, then months, I watched my children play on the other side of closed windows, while I lay in bed listening to the whirr of my portable air filter and gripping my red inhaler. In every sense, I needed a new breath of life, and I needed it desperately. Our conversations, Jonathan's and mine, became prayers: *Lord, lead us on. We want to breathe deeply again. We want to raise four children in a rambling farmhouse where we can make room for guests and friends and chickens and gardens. We want to move on, but we want it to feel like return.*

Newly conceived desires grew, keeping pace with a growing baby. Yet I am still uncertain: Did we ask for Maplehurst? Did we ask to trade longleaf pines for deciduous maples? Did the dream come from within us, or was it somehow given to us? If it did come from within, it only emerged, only became visible, when the forest we had always lived in, the forest of our plans and aspirations, burned away. What remained was rooted in a past we had either forgotten or only ever known secondhand: my great-grandmother's flower garden, the family farm with its pecan orchard, my father's fruit trees, and the remains of a nineteenth-century, citrus-growing homestead. Florida was a wildfire in my life, but today I say thank you for the very place that once snatched my breath away.

There are few remaining traces of one of the most important trees that ever grew in North America: *Castanea dentata*, the American chestnut. Mark Hughes would have watched it flower in the forests around his fields in Pennsylvania. Citrus farmers in northern Florida would have known the rich taste of its fruit. Treasured by urban elites and Appalachian poor alike, chestnut trees bloomed in summer and hung heavy with food (and a cash crop) in fall. As one mountain dweller put it, chestnuts "were like the manna that God sent to feed the Israelites."[4] But if the story of manna, the bread of heaven, is told and retold, remembered and passed on, we have largely failed to tell the story of *Castanea dentata*, the species that once dominated the hardwood forests of the east.

Scientists estimate that at one time, nearly 20 percent of the trees east of the Mississippi River were chestnut trees, and in some portions of the Appalachians, pure chestnut forests grew for mile after mile. Chestnut trees were such a majestic cornerstone of eastern landscapes and chestnut wood was so ubiquitous in fencing, furniture-making, and railroads that, as one historian memorably tells it, "Americans rode on chestnut-paneled trains running along chestnut rail ties to reach jobs behind chestnut desks to receive messages transmitted over chestnut utility poles. They dined on chestnut stuffing at chestnut tables while wearing leather clothes tanned with chestnut."[5] But in the summer of

1904, the leaves on chestnut trees growing in New York began to wither and brown. Later, the culprit would be traced to a fungus that had arrived with nursery stock from Japan. By the middle of the century, and despite herculean efforts to stop it, the fungus had covered 200 million acres and wiped out virtually every mature specimen of this beloved tree. Somewhere between 3 and 4 billion chestnut trees were lost.

The vanished chestnut trees left their trace at Maplehurst, but I would never have seen it if it hadn't been for a skilled home repairman named Bill. I contacted him after searching for an old home restorer on a local online message board, and not so long ago, he stopped by to look at our house. Like the handyman who had previously visited, Bill didn't say much at first, but he seemed willing to take a look at everything. I showed him the inside and the outside of the house, wishing the entire time that I could read his thoughts. At least the advertising catchphrase on his truck was encouraging: "Breathing New Life into Historic Homes." It made me think of breathing trees and the breath of life and the asthma that had quietly slipped away, for good, on the morning Elsa was born, though I did not mention any of that to Bill.

When we found ourselves back out on the lawn, Bill poked his head into the dark interior of the red shed that abuts our vegetable garden. "Do you know when this was built?" he asked.

"I don't," I said. "But I've always been afraid it will tumble down on our heads. Maybe it was added when the stone bank barn caved in? We have paperwork that says the barn fell down in 1980."

"That makes sense," he said. "They may have salvaged some wood from the barn to build this shed. Do you see this beam?"

I stepped closer and peered into the dim corners of the building my kids insist on calling a barn but I'm too embarrassed to call anything more than a shed, and I noticed for the first time the very long wooden beam supporting the rafters beneath the metal roof.

"Yes?"

"That is a single piece of wood. Too long to be anything but chestnut. And those trees disappeared a long, long time ago."

Then I understood, not because I knew much at all about American chestnut trees, but because I remembered a painting from 1906 by N. C. Wyeth called *The Last of the Chestnuts*. It shows two men who have been chopping and stacking lumber, but they are dwarfed by an enormous tree stump in the foreground of the picture. Long shadows and autumnal colors give the whole painting an elegiac atmosphere. Both men hold axes, but they have paused in their work and their heads are bowed as if in prayer or perhaps mourning. I know the painting because the Wyeths are a local family, and a famous one. N. C. Wyeth (1882–1945) was known for his illustrations and the cover designs he painted for books such as Robert Louis Stephenson's *Treasure Island*. His son Andrew Wyeth (1917–2009) is best remembered for his moody and mysterious masterpiece *Christina's World*. Andrew's son Jamie, now in his seventies, is also a well-known painter, the latest heir to the Brandywine School of artists begun with N. C.'s teacher, Howard Pyle. Memory and memorial are themes in the art created by all three generations, and one of the first substantial paintings Andrew completed was called *The Chestnut Tree*. The disappearance of the chestnut trees has been called "one of the worst ecological disasters in the nation's history,"[6] and in a 1916 letter, N.C. Wyeth wrote of the loss, "It makes me sick to think of it."[7] When Bill pointed out our chestnut beam, I felt as if I had been told that a ghost was holding up the roof of our old red shed.

❦

The landscape around Maplehurst and all along the Brandywine River is a haunted landscape. It's not uncommon for Revolutionary War-and Civil War-era cannonballs to be dug up in suburban backyards and construction sites. Place names like "New London" and "London Grove" go on repeating the aspirations and the homesickness of colonial newcomers. The voices of even older communities are heard in place names like Toughkenamon and Wissinoming. Crumbling yet unyielding stone walls mark boundaries first drawn in William Penn's day, and secret staircases and hidden closets remember the songs and sorrows of runaway slaves. Though the past is unavoidable here, no place is a blank slate, and memory may be just as necessary for placemaking as vision. If it is possible to cultivate peace on the earth, it may be that this is only possible by cultivating memory. One of the greatest promises of Scripture is that even the very ends of the earth will remember and so return to the Lord.[8] We cannot make a place new without attending to what it has been. We need history books. We need to listen to our older neighbors. We need to open our eyes and seek out the traces of what remains.

I encounter one particular ghost every Sunday on our drive to and from church. I have named it the "ghost avenue," and there must be others like it. It is all that is left of what must once have been a long, tree-lined drive like the one that leads to my own front door. In the middle of a large county park, two parallel rows of tall but twisted sycamore trees meander from nowhere to nowhere in a gentle curve. They lift ghostly white limbs to the sky, but the road between these trees has disappeared. There is now little more than a depression in the grass strewn with gravel. Once, a family must have passed beneath these limbs on every journey home, but that home has vanished, and only the sycamores testify to its vanishing. I am not sure whether the ghost avenue frightens me or only makes me sad. But every Sunday, it reminds me of the fragility of my own old home with its avenue of trees. It reminds me how ephemeral even a house can be. Despite its broken bricks and decaying woodwork, Maplehurst seems too solid ever to be erased, yet those sycamores once led the way to a farmhouse that must have appeared just as enduring.

We cannot make a place new without attending to what it has been.

Farmhouses persist and farmhouses fade, and I wonder if I am fighting a losing battle at Maplehurst with time and decay and the fragility even of living memory. I failed to remember the dramatic crape myrtles of my hometown. Few today remember the manna that was the American chestnut. Why should we pay attention to the traces of the past that still mark a place? Is it only nostalgia and sentiment that keeps me captivated by places that have passed and are every day passing away? The history of the American chestnut is an ecological cautionary tale, but I think it is more than that. I know when Bill first pointed out our chestnut beam, my heart leapt, and I think it leapt for joy. That beam embodies the persistence of the past. It looks to me like a promise that the good things of the past are not all doomed to disappear. The promise of the past can be fulfilled. Renewal and restoration are possible.

Someone once cared enough to salvage that beam from the wreck of the barn. They didn't give in to hopelessness, and the work of their hands endures. I thought the red shed was ready to buckle, but Bill said it still has a lot of life left in it. "There's nothing like a chestnut beam," he said. One day, if the shed doesn't fall down on its own, with Bill's help we might take it down, dismantle it carefully, and preserve the chestnut beam. We'll build a new barn, not a shed, but a structure we will all be proud to call a barn, and the roof will be held up by a survivor. Beneath that beam, we'll host gatherings and retreats and writing workshops and goodness even knows what else. Perhaps my daughters, maybe even my sons, will celebrate marriages there one day. Three born in Chicago and one, Elsa, born to Maplehurst in Pennsylvania.

Remembering Florida, I've remembered the pleasure of making a place beautiful simply for the sake of beauty. And the light in Bill's eyes when we shook hands told me he knows this joy too. "I've been praying God would bring me another old house to restore," he said. And then he told me, with a smile, to call him Dr. Bill. "I'm a doctor of old houses," he said, and my knees buckled a little bit when I realized that what Maplehurst needs is exactly what each of us needs: a healer.

When we first arrived, Jonathan and I imagined transforming this place all on our own. We'd been doing everything on our own for a few years by then, as if we'd forgotten all the lessons the city had taught us. But now I understood that our neighbor, John, would restore the windows, and Bill, who lives in his own very old house not far north of us, would restore everything else, and Jonathan and I would go on building gardens and planting trees. I don't know exactly how we'll pay for it, but lately I am buoyed by a kind of irrational hope.

Our Florida years were a season of heartache, and I would never want to live them again. Yet the residue of my memories—the thing that remains and endures—isn't really sadness at all. It is joy. The joy of finally—*finally!*—embarking on the long road home. Of course, that road was lined with trees. Longleaf pines with deadly pollen. Forgotten crape myrtles with flowers like bursts of light. Chestnuts, beloved of artists and remembered by craftspeople. Orange trees with flowers like starlight and fruit like sunshine. And maples. Norway maples. Silver maples. Maple trees like lanterns, leading the way.

Chapter 9

Silver Maple

THE PRICE OF A PLACE

Placemaking requires more than the proverbial drama of blood, sweat, and tears. It also asks for something as ordinary and unimaginative as money. The God who sends dreams and the God who desires the praise of trees guided us to Maplehurst, and though the needs of this place are greater than we anticipated, I believe that this same God will provide. Even so, belief does not erase all my worries or answer all of my self-doubts. How will we pay for the work we know must be done? And even if the money can be found, how can we justify spending so much on bricks and mortar and window glass? These questions are a fog my eyes can't penetrate.

Until I remember the trees.

Maplehurst is named for the silver maples lining both sides of the long driveway and the giant Norway maples nearer to the house. I knew little about maple trees before moving here. I have learned you can tap any variety of maple for syrup, though the aptly named sugar maples do give the highest concentration of sugary sap. I have learned Norway maples are considered invasive. Though they were enormously popular as fast-growing yard trees 100 years ago, Norway maples launch a voluminous amount of the winged maple seeds known as samaras, and they cast these helicopters far and wide. The Norway maple's dense canopy, while providing lovely shade for outdoor meals with friends, makes it difficult for native species to thrive beneath their branches. I have also learned that maples are the fastest growing of the hardwood trees. This may sound like a good thing, but it means their wood is often weak. Quite unlike the white oak tree near our house that has danced in place for almost 400 years, the average lifespan of a silver maple is 100 years. Though Norway maples may live longer, they seldom do. In other words, one of the most important things I have learned is that our trees are dying. Planted when this home was fresh and new, they are crumbling almost in lockstep with the mortar and the soffits.

We had lived at Maplehurst only a few months when we awoke one morning to the sight of a giant maple lying stricken across our lawn. It looked as if the wind had twisted the trunk and gone on twisting it until the venerable tree had finally given up and released its grip on its own roots. We knew our trees were big, but we did not know how big until we stood in the shadow of that great, fallen tree. Even sprawled on its side, the trunk was so high above my head I could not climb it without a great helping heave from Jonathan. Our first spring in the house was an especially stormy one, and the trees seemed to drop bits and pieces of themselves in every breeze. Fortunately, most of our trees grow at quite a distance from our roof, but after one fierce fifteen-minute deluge, we found an enormous limb, nearly one-third of the tree itself, fallen across our driveway. It was shocking to realize how easily our only access to the street could become impassable, but it was more stunning to see that the maple's huge, reaching limb was nearly hollow, rotted out from the inside. Maple trees do not die the way people do. The older they grow, the more majestic they become, but that majesty is deceptive. Inwardly, they carry their age in rotten wood and hollow hearts. They decay from the inside out.

Our maple trees were a bonus in the real estate agent's brochure, and I accepted them as a gift from heaven until they began to cost a great deal of time and money. The first check I wrote to the owner of a local tree-care company felt inevitable. There are always hidden costs to home ownership. I wrote the second check a little more slowly. But the third lay unsigned on my desk for days. Unlike the others, this check was for tree care rather than cleanup. The price tag was alarming, but the promise was enticing. If we were willing to pay the cost equivalent of a small used vehicle, this company could prune every one of our aging trees. With knowledge, experience, and a great deal of heavy equipment, they could remove dead wood and too-heavy branches. With fewer limbs—and fewer leaves—these trees might persist, despite their age and weakness, despite the inevitable storms.

But were we willing to pay the price? For *trees*?

A storm-wrecked tree falls on a driveway, and we call it a sorrow and an affliction. A storm-wrecked tree crashes onto the forest floor, and scientists call it a fiercely generative gift. When a forest tree falls, it tears a hole in the forest's leafy canopy. The combination of fresh sunlight and broken wood is combustible, but it burns with a life-giving flame. Within hours of a tree's collapse, the sugary reek of ruined wood has gathered to itself beetles and other insects that chew and bore. Singing birds will come; silent bacteria will come. Various fungi will flower and ooze. Larvae and maggots will grow in the rainwater puddles that collect in every dip and hollow of the fallen trunk. Furry mammals, drawn by sunshine and a dry lookout, will deposit seeds in and around the tree right along with the fertilizer needed for growth. Scientist David George Haskell tells us that "at least half of the other species in the forest find food or home in or on the recumbent bodies of fallen trees."[1] Trees find a second life in the rot that follows death. Forests are messy, and their future lies in the mess.

There are broken and fallen trees on the edges of our property at Maplehurst that we will never clean up. These are trees that may once have been planted, but more likely they sprouted and grew in a thicket and were intentionally untended to serve as a windbreak. Beneath the shade of tall silver maples, these edges are a mess of dead branches, wineberry canes, poison ivy, and thorny wild roses. There are aggressive wild grape vines and more decorous yet still invasive porcelain-berry vines whose fruit resembles exquisite painted-blue china. And dotted throughout are signs of cultivated plantings that either predate the windbreak or, more likely, stand as testaments to the gardeners who have tried and failed to clean up these wild ribbons in the land. When I pick wineberries with Elsa in June, I often find hostas half-buried by vines and raggedy azalea shrubs starved for sunshine.

I'd trade these brambly edges for a neat woodland garden stocked with precious native plants in a heartbeat, but I have neither the time nor the energy to cultivate them, and my better self knows that wildness serves a purpose. Not only do the messy, unpruned trees provide a better windbreak for the house, but in a landscape of neat suburban yards, Maplehurst's chaotic borders also provide a rare habitat for birds, insects, and small mammals—not to mention a convenient spot to toss dried Christmas trees and moldy porch pumpkins. The silver maples lining our driveway are different; they are less wild and more domesticated. Planted by a visionary hand a century or more ago, these trees are part of an artistic design, and our appreciation of their artistry comes with the responsibility to care for them, to clean up after them, and to replant the gap they leave when they fall. The silver maples along our driveway are no longer forest trees; they are garden trees.

If gardening is the domestication of nature, then gardening is always more of a dream and a far-off goal than a reality. In my garden, I dream of order and perfection, but I cultivate chaos. Every winter, I forget that this is the way of things. For a few months, I believe what the photographs in my gardening books seem to say: that gardening is neat rows of baby lettuces or a climbing rose in perfumed abundance. Of course, it *is* those things, but only for five minutes. Turn your back and the lettuces have bolted, becoming bitter in their rush to produce seed. Blink your eyes and the rose is covered in beetles, or a maple has dropped another limb. Even every sweet, sun-warmed strawberry is teetering on the edge of rot.

In July and August, I teeter on the edge of grateful and overwhelmed as I rush between the garden and the kitchen. Gardening depends on the kitchen, because plants do not produce food in the exact proportions needed for our nightly suppers. In the summer garden's ridiculous extravagance, we find the explanation for everything from grain barns to root cellars to modern tin cans and deep freezers. Summer overdoes it because winter, at least in Pennsylvania, will have nothing to do with growing food. Still, I can forget that my work is not finished when I snap a pea or pull a carrot. I forget until an awful smell in the refrigerator reminds me of my neglect. A grocery-store lettuce left to liquefy in a crisper bin is a mess, but a seed-grown "Crisp Mint" garden romaine abandoned to the same fate is a tragedy. Alas, this tragedy runs local performances in my yard and kitchen all summer long. In the morning, I pick a bowl of perfectly petite cucumbers, and at night I return to find terrifying monster cucumbers lurking beneath the leaves. How did I miss them? Could they have grown so much in a day?

I try to reassure myself. *They are only vegetables; this is not the end of the world.* And yet there are too many days when it feels like exactly that. As if overgrown vegetables are only the first sign of the mortal chaos that threatens everything. Cucumbers never stop growing, and this old house never stops crumbling, and my children never stop changing, and I never manage to quite catch up on everything I think must be done. I never manage to hold and keep and preserve the things that matter most. But I try.

My favorite method for preserving the garden harvest is fermentation, a process that dances perilously close to the line between ripe and rotten. For thousands of years, humans have harnessed the bacteria naturally present in air and on the surface of food to transform perishable produce into something longer lasting, more delicious, and more nutritious. Before the relatively recent invention of water-bath canning, every dill pickle was a lacto-fermented pickle. In other words, it was alive the way a fallen log on the forest floor is alive. Food and garden writer Michael Pollan describes as "startling" the recent medical discovery that "in order to be healthy, people need *more* exposure to microbes, not less . . . Bacteria-free food," he writes, "may be making us sick."[2] But the fear of bacteria that first took hold in the nineteenth century is now deeply ingrained in us. We have largely abandoned the fermented foods that filled our bellies in the days before freezers and antibacterial soaps.

I like that my old-fashioned pickles are healthier, but I love that they do not require me to tend a pot of boiling water in my hot summer kitchen. Instead, I combine cucumbers and salt-water, along with whole garlic cloves and fresh dill, and leave them to bubble in jars in the cool spot on my cellar steps. In only a few days, I have crisp, tangy pickles. Is it possible then to harness decay? In yogurt, kombucha tea, and sourdough bread, is it possible to arrest the march toward chaos and death? Not always. Bacteria are living organisms. Like people, they are unpredictable. Sometimes, for reasons I can never fathom, my sauerkraut grows mold or my kombucha refuses to fizz. But failure sweetens the taste of success. Because I cannot entirely control the process, the transformation of cucumber to pickle is always a delightfully anticipated surprise. No matter how many jars I store in the cool cave of our home's old root cellar, I can never forget this truth: each and every bite is a miracle and a gift.

Still, there are days. Days when I am overwhelmed by the sun-ripened tomatoes turning into puddles on my counter. Days when the same rain that feeds the growing apples on our trees also breaks through the plaster ceiling of our kitchen. Days when trees fall and chaos and decay seem to reign. These are the days I wish I, too, could dance on that line between ripe and rotten. Instead, I tend to lie down, pull the covers over my head, and wish for bedtime. In my dreams, nothing ever rots or wilts or grows unmanageable. In my dreams, even the children I longed for so desperately grow small again. I wake and remember what it was like when I could hold them completely within the small circle of my lap.

I could can all of it. The cucumbers, the cabbages, the apples. I could boil them in a churning pot until I'd killed every last microbe with an urge toward contamination. I could line up super-sealed jars on my pantry shelves and never worry about mold. I could probably find a way to heat-treat everything else as well. Not only my food, but my yard and this house and my relationships. I could boil my garden vegetables, toss our old windows in a dumpster, ignore the oak tree on the golf course, and distance myself from friends and family and neighbors. I could fence in my children with a hundred thousand rules. Then they would be safe. Then they would be contained. Then they would no longer have the opportunity to break

Dead things are risk-free and easy to manage, but can they feed the soul?

my heart. Dead things are risk-free and easy to manage, but can they feed the soul? If I want a home that is alive, I think I must accept the chaos of its living.

❧

Unlike Maplehurst, our Florida home did not teem with life. When my vegetable seedlings withered in the heat, when wildfire smoke imprisoned us indoors, I reminded myself that Jonathan's job in Florida was always meant to be temporary. Two or three years at most, we had been told, and then he would be offered a transfer somewhere else. We were both hanging our hopes on the idea of that transfer, but we didn't merely want to move away from Florida; we wanted to move *toward* the things we had only begun to glimpse in dreams: a spacious place where friends and neighbors could gather, where peace could grow as surely as apple trees. We hoped for a place where those in need of a home could find one with our family and where the weary might come for a day, or even a season, of rest. This isn't the kind of list you hand to a real estate agent. So we waited. And we trusted. But as my belly grew, our hope of finding this special place before our daughter was born began to seem more and more impossible. When Jonathan asked his superiors about the promised transfer, they said, "We have something in mind for you in upstate New York. Nothing is settled yet. We'll let you know soon."

Elsa was due to be born in September. In late April, I began to unpack and wash the tiny pink sweaters and caps I had stored away assuming I would only pull them out for a granddaughter one day. In May, I began to feel yet another hot Florida summer closing in around me. The tree pollen had dissipated, but my breathing had only slightly improved. I comforted myself with dreams of upstate New York, a place I had never even visited let alone imagined living in. But the idea of New York, so unknown and so far from any family or friends, also terrified me. I was reminded of the tiny newborn chick in the book I sometimes read to Beau. Just hatched from his egg, he wanders around asking everything from a cow to an airplane, "Are you my mother?" I thought of New York and wondered, *Are you my home?* But I heard no answer. On days when hope felt as difficult as breath, I flipped pages in my Bible in a daze. Near the middle of June, I wrenched my Bible open in despair, almost daring a silent and invisible God to speak to me. Immediately, I saw these words: "Daughter Zion . . . he will not prolong your exile."[3]

A week later, Jonathan called from a business trip. "I've been offered a position at company headquarters in Wilmington, Delaware," he said. My breath became tangled in surprise and confusion. "What happened to New York?" I gasped.

"I have no idea," he said.

"You've been there before for meetings. Is Delaware nice?" I asked.

"Well," he said slowly. "I guess I've never seen much of it beyond the office." I felt my vision of New England evaporate, a vision that had dovetailed so well with the farmhouse photo I had clipped from that magazine. Instead of New York, I had a place name—Delaware—that meant nothing to me. Only a blank where I hoped our home would be.

One of the questions we hear most frequently from those who visit us at Maplehurst is "How did you find this place?" The unspoken subtext seems to be that this farmhouse planted right in the middle of suburbia is unique, yet well suited to us. The questioners are right in that assumption. In Florida we began to dream of a farmhouse with room for the animals and gardens that would help us find new meaning and purpose for our home, but we also dreamed of community such as we had known in Chicago and grieved the loss of in Florida. In our imaginations, we could never reconcile those two things: how could we live in a country home yet cultivate community? There may be as many ways to do that as there are places, yet we couldn't clearly see a single one until the day we found Maplehurst: a farmhouse in a neighborhood, a country house in suburbia. In between and exactly right.

We said yes to Delaware. I hadn't yet heard the local joke— "Dela-where?"—but it would have made sense to me. We really had no idea where we were headed, but we drew a twenty-mile line from Jonathan's Delaware office away from the flatter, coastal land toward the neighboring hills of Pennsylvania, put our Florida home on the market, left our children in the care of their grandparents, and flew to Philadelphia to spend the Fourth of July looking for home. We gave our real estate agent the parameters that would considerably narrow our list: old house, many bedrooms, a few acres, and most of all, affordable. Only eight properties made the cut and half of those just barely. On one of the hottest days of the year, we drove down a long, long driveway beneath the fluttering silver leaves of so many trees.

The maple trees that had inspired the home's name more than a hundred years before were the first to greet us. Like an arboreal welcoming committee, they lined the long avenue that linked the country road with the home's front porch. The trees tossed their leaves, but I strained my eyes to peer through their branches, eager to see just how near our nearest human neighbors were. I saw the giant trees, yet I did not see them. They were simply the backdrop for the good things I hoped God would do in this place. Though Maplehurst is a farmhouse, the farm itself was sold for development years ago. That first day, we could hear Amish carpenters tapping nails into the last of the new homes being built nearby. The proximity of so many neighbors was a real estate liability, but we saw in it an answer to prayer. Our dream of a farmhouse purposed for community had never made much sense until we saw all those houses planted where Guernsey cattle had once wandered alongside fields planted by local commercial rose growers. Obviously, if God was bringing us here, he was bringing us here for the people. I never once suspected he might be bringing us here for the trees.

I have two other stories about why we chose this place, but I rarely share them. The first is too personal, the second too mysterious—and both are a little hard for even me to believe. When we first stepped over the threshold at Maplehurst on that steamy July day, I found papers lying neatly on a desk in the parlor. One of them showed a list of Maplehurst's previous owners. It was not a long list, and on that list I found my father's family's name: Day. Fifty years before, Maplehurst had been purchased by a man named Charles Day, and though it seems this branch of the Day family has little more than a tenuous link with the Days of Comanche County, Texas, for me it was a sign of homecoming.

Only a few weeks before, my friend Melissa, who would be among our first visitors, called and told me she had dreamed that she came to visit me at my new house.

"What was it like?" I asked with a laugh.

Her tone of voice in response was serious. She knew, I suppose, that dream details are sometimes a little too specific. Sharing them with me might only make it harder for us to choose the right place.

"I couldn't see the house clearly," she said quietly, "but it had a very long driveway, and it had many, many trees. I thought I heard the trees whispering a word."

"What word?" I asked, my own voice quieter now.

"Jubilee."

Trees are not widows and orphans. Trees are not the ministry of the church. Yet trees spread their roots throughout the stories the Bible tells. Adam and Eve broke their close connection with their maker beneath the heavy-laden branches of a fruit tree. A felled tree held Jesus, the woodworker from Nazareth, as he died. In the Bible's closing chapters, we read about the day when heaven and earth will be joined, and we will live beneath the shelter of a marvelous healing tree.[4] In Scripture, the trees praise God.[5] Do they not know that their days are numbered? Do the trees not understand that one day their home, this earth, "will wear out like a garment"?[6]

Having chosen Maplehurst—because we believed it had been chosen for us—I wondered for the first time in my life about the value of a tree beyond its beauty or its shade. Certainly, trees are the lungs of the earth. Without the oxygen released by trees, we couldn't sing God's praises, and my own lungs and those of my children have shown themselves to be especially vulnerable. But it was only after I became intimately acquainted with bark and roots and leaves here at Maplehurst that I realized these biblical trees had always been paper-thin in my mind. Mere metaphors. Even the fig tree cursed by Jesus was little more than an insubstantial object lesson. But despite the flimsiness of the paper check awaiting signature on my desk, I was not being asked to pay metaphorical money for my Maplehurst trees. The cash we might spend on these old maples was cold and hard, and I could think of a dozen more "spiritual" ways it might be used. Even leaving that aspect aside, I could more easily justify making a deposit in my children's meager college savings accounts, or paying for any of the needed house repairs, than spending one more penny on these dying trees. Yet, as pastor Adele Calhoun writes, "Trees carry theology in their veins."[7] I had never reckoned the full worth of a tree.

I wrote the third check. I wrote it though I had not resolved my doubts. I wrote it only because I decided that if the cattle on a thousand hills belong to our God, then surely there is enough divine bounty for both orphans *and* trees. But it was only after the pruning was finished that I began to comprehend the opportunity we had been given. The "limbing up" of our trees took two full days and a large crew of hard-hatted men. By early evening on the second day, we had three enormous piles of fresh mulch for the garden, but we had something more too. As the last truck rolled back down the drive, Jonathan and I stood side by side on the front porch. Where an impenetrable green curtain had only days ago rippled in the breeze, our eyes now traveled the full length of the driveway. Two days before, it had looked like a long, dark tunnel. Now it was like a soaring cathedral of light. With their heavy lower limbs removed, our trees appeared to touch the sky. Silvery green leaves met above the driveway in a vast, delicate arch. "I had no idea they were so tall," Jonathan whispered.

Three years have passed since that day, and we have not lost another tree.

This earth often looks like a patched and faded garment, just as the prophet Isaiah predicted. Nations rage. Neighbors squabble. My apple trees are stricken with blight. Even these maple trees will not stand forever, no matter how well we care for them. Why, then, do they sing? And why should we join their chorus? I had no vision for how beautiful our old trees could be. With my eyes clouded by dollar signs, I'd thought only of their aging wood and drooping limbs. If it had been possible, I might have tossed them in a garbage can the way I dispose of a pair of ragged old jeans. St. Paul told us that all the invisible attributes of God are made visible in creation.[8] Though our trees were planted by men and women, they were created to reflect God's glory. Even I could see that now. And I had been invited to participate in the glory, called to cultivate and care for these towering blessings, and thus, to share in the peace of their shelter. I originally thought the amount on that third check such a high price to pay, but now I considered it a bargain.

I came to Maplehurst with a heart to care for people, but God wanted more from me. God wanted more *for* me. He wanted to bring me into a community, not only with people, but also with all of creation. Maple trees and daffodils, blue skies and star-

In so many ways, and with our participation, this earth is being remade from the inside out.

light. Incredible gifts like these should never become mere backdrop. We sing with the trees because death and decay met their defeat on a wooden cross. We sing because Isaiah also spoke of a new earth that would "endure."[9] I don't know exactly when or how that forever earth will come to be, but I feel sure that I have glimpsed it. I see it in every strong, young red maple planted where an old, decaying silver maple once grew. I see it when neighbors gather to hunt Easter eggs beneath a cathedral arch of rejuvenated trees. And I begin to suspect that in so many ways, and with our participation, this earth is being remade from the inside out.

As are we.

Maplehurst, too, is being restored from the inside out, though I was not prepared for all that would be revealed. Soon after he began his work here, Bill, our doctor of old houses, the healer on whom we have pinned our hopes for this place, called me over to look at something on the southeast corner of the house. He had been busy that day digging out rotten wood, and as I watched a pile of tattered shards and fragments grow (along with the size of a new hole in our roofline), I felt my hopes deflate. So far, I had only let myself imagine fresh new wood and gleaming white paint, but I was beginning to realize that our house would look much worse before it began to look better. "Take a look at this," Bill called to me. I walked over and stood beneath the roof of the kitchen addition that juts out on the southern side of the house.

"I see a hole?" I called back.

"That's right," said Dr. Bill, "a hole. The rafters holding up your roof in this spot should be resting on a beam. But the beam is gone. This end of it has rotted right away."

I said nothing. Merely stared at that place where load-bearing wood had silently decayed until, splinter by splinter, it had vanished. "Oh, Bill," I finally said.

"I know, I know," the doctor said. "We're beginning this work just in time. I have a length of reclaimed chestnut at my place. I'll fit in a new beam tomorrow."

Rot. I hate the sound of that word. I hate even the feel of it in my mouth. But I am no longer sure exactly what it signifies. Death? Life? Where does one end and the other begin? I am tempted to lump decay and death together, but the life of a fallen forest tree or the fermentation I practice in the kitchen defy this easy categorization. It is a tangle as intricate and messy and abundant as the overgrown edges of this place. For now, I find hope in the words of the English poet George Meredith:

> *Earth knows no desolation.*
> *She smells regeneration*
> *In the moist breath of decay.*[10]

Chapter 10

Norway Maple

PLACEMAKING AROUND
THE TABLE

I have written of these many places Jonathan and I have called home primarily through a view of trees. I have done so because most trees are longer lived than we, and they seem at once unchanging yet also particularly vulnerable. They are vulnerable to disease and pests as well as the colonist's axe and the developer's bulldozer. They are vulnerable to our neglect, but they also suffer under our attention. Their presence and their absence testify to the ways we both make and unmake the land around us.

But trees can have a long and happy afterlife, and I might have described the same places with stories of warm wooden tables and sturdy wooden chairs. Not the oak on the golf course behind Maplehurst, but the oak of the round pedestal table we bought in an antique store as newlyweds. Not the longleaf pines of Florida, but the pinewood of the long rectangular table we first bought for the formal dining room at Eaton Place. In other words, I could tell the story of a place from the point of view of the old wooden dining chairs we've used in every kitchen, dining nook, and dining room where we've ever set our table. Jonathan has recovered the fabric seats of those chairs three times since we bought them secondhand in Texas. These chairs and these tables are a continuous link between all the places we have made. They are solid wood to the ephemeral spring blossoms of the meals and moments, the parties and the gatherings held around them.

We hadn't even unpacked all of our boxes, Elsa hadn't even yet been born, when we hosted our first large gathering at Maplehurst. Shortly before our move from Florida, my friend Aimee from Chicago called to say that she and her husband Rand and their three children would be attending a wedding in Pennsylvania's Lancaster County in August. Could they possibly come stay with us after the event? Our answer was yes. Then we called Nathan and Melissa, good friends from Chicago who also loved Rand and Aimee. Nathan and Melissa had recently relocated to Maryland with their two sons, and Melissa's own baby girl was due to be born not long after Elsa. Would they come up for a small reunion of Chicago friends? Their answer was yes. And that is why one of the first things we did after arriving at Maplehurst was load our car with three children and my pregnant bulk and drive an hour to the nearest IKEA. We needed a queen-sized guest bed that wouldn't require a box spring for one of the third-floor bedrooms. We had brought a spare mattress from our Florida home when we moved in the week before, but then we discovered that the box spring wouldn't fit up the winding back stairs that joined the second floor with the third. At IKEA, we found a bed frame in white metal with a slatted wood base designed to support a mattress without the need for a bulky box spring. We carried it in pieces up the stairs before squishing the top mattress up behind it. We had a thousand other things to do, but hospitality was our priority for this place, and we tackled preparations for our first gathering like new farmers who've turned a calendar page and suddenly realized it's planting time.

The glass dining table from our Florida patio had immediately found a home on the wide front porch at Maplehurst, but with eight children among our three families, we needed more seats for summer's outdoor meals. The previous owners had left an old wooden picnic table with a bench and several chairs sitting beneath the limbs of the largest Norway maple in the yard, but they had left it only after asking our permission and with apologies. The set was so encrusted with lichen and moss that it looked to me more ornamental than functional, but Jonathan saw what I could not. He pulled out his power washer, and for several hours, while I grumbled quietly about the boxes he was not unpacking and the photographs he was not helping me hang, he transformed that outdoor picnic set. If this were a different sort of book, you would find here two full-color photographs, one labeled *before* and the other *after*, and you would stare in awed disbelief.

I don't remember much from that first Maplehurst gathering, but I do remember how we sat around the gleaming wood of our remade, hand-me-down table eating bacon, lettuce, and tomato sandwiches in the shade beneath the Norway maple. Aimee and Melissa had rescued the tomatoes from the overgrown vegetable garden next to the dilapidated red shed. The previous owner had planted them before she realized her home would sell that same summer, and she would have no time for weeding. Ever since, the children who were with us that day have referred to

Maplehurst as "the bacon house," because, while we adults ate our sandwiches, the kids helped themselves to every last strip of bacon we had left in the kitchen for second servings. When Rand ventured back to the house to make another sandwich, he found the platters licked clean and the children nowhere to be found.

It is often children who stumble on just the right name for a place. I have heard other children call Maplehurst "the apple house" (those particular children helped me pick apples from our trees last September), and still others have called it "the pizza house" (those children used to join us for our Friday night tradition of homemade pizza). Other than my friend Aimee's thrill-seeking son, who insists on calling our home the "zipline house," these names all come back to food. We receive more than vitamins and nutrients when we eat. We also receive the intangible things that make a place a place: its flavor, its perfume, its music, its people. We taste, we talk, we share, and a place comes alive and reveals new dimensions of itself. For one special family, ours is the house where, together, we have enjoyed the best food of our lives. The best food, of course, is not only the most delicious, it is nourishing in ways that go far deeper than taste buds and appetite. The best food satisfies all kinds of hunger.

If Chicago tasted like deep-dish pizza, and if Florida tasted like local Mayport shrimp, then Maplehurst tastes like corn on the cob so sweet I no longer bother with butter. The area around our home has some of the most fertile

> *We receive more than vitamins and nutrients when we eat. We also receive the intangible things that make a place a place: its flavor, its perfume, its music, its people. We taste, we talk, we share, and a place comes alive and reveals new dimensions of itself.*

agricultural land in the country and no need for irrigation, and the local Amish farmers as well as other growers take full advantage of these conditions. When my father, who has lived in Midwestern farm country for years now, drove the backroads with me during a visit last September, he told me he'd never seen such tall corn stalks. He could hardly believe they grew only on rainwater. But my favorite local flavor may be the August melons, enormous cantaloupes with a sugary-sweet smell, and compact watermelons with dark green rinds and vivid pink hearts. Those watermelons are so delicious, my friend Nara once bought one from a nearby farmstand on the last day of her visit and carried it on her lap for her flight to California. California may grow most of our country's produce, but Nara said no one in her family there would ever have tasted a melon so sweet.

We met Nara and her husband, Scott, during our first year in Chicago. We kept in touch only intermittently after they moved away and as our families grew, but we corresponded more frequently by email once we knew that our sons, her Josh and my Thaddeus, suffered from the same life-threatening food allergies. When Scott and Nara and their two daughters and son moved to Tokyo, Japan, I assumed our friendship would remain email-only, but Nara surprised me not long after our move to Maplehurst when she asked whether she could bring her kids for a week-long summer stay. "We'll fit it in between a visit with my family in Chicago and a visit with Scott's family in California," she explained. "Scott has work in New York that week, but I'd like our boys to know one another. I'd like my son to know he's not the only one who can't eat bread or ice cream or peanut butter."

This would be our first full summer at Maplehurst, and the house did not seem ready for such ambitious hospitality. There was no air conditioning, and heat waves are always a possibility here in summer. The windows in the third-floor bedrooms were especially rickety and rotten, liable to shed flakes of lead-based paint when opened. But perhaps I was the one who didn't feel ready. Settling into this new place and caring for three young children and an infant while Jonathan traveled extensively for his new job had stretched me thin. Our home had plenty of extra bedrooms, but I felt emptied out, like I had nothing left to give. The anxiety that first flooded my mind after Elsa's birth simmered up again: *What if the children don't get along? What if the weather is too hot and humid to sleep comfortably on the third floor? What if I make some mistake in the kitchen and Josh has an allergic reaction? What if? What if? What if?*

During the weekend of the bacon escapade, our friend Rand kept repeating the same question: "Where am I, exactly?" He was a California transplant who had made Chicago home for many years, and though he had driven east from Chicago before wandering down through Lancaster County toward Maplehurst, he struggled to place himself in this landscape where cities, suburbs, and farms, including quite a few tree farms, lay in such bewildering proximity to one another. Jonathan and I were so new to the area that we struggled to answer his question. But even now, several years later, it is a question I still wrestle with. Where is Maplehurst? With towns and cities, farms and suburbs so near and so interwoven, this has remained a surprisingly knotty question. It is a puzzle even technology cannot solve: our mailing address here at Maplehurst includes the name of the small borough that lies two miles to our west, while all of the internet mapping services insist on using the name of the equally small borough two miles to our east. I thought I felt ill at ease in suburban Florida because it was neither one thing nor the other, neither the city I had loved and left nor the country I glimpsed from the front porch at Alpine Groves Park. At Maplehurst, a version of this awkward in-betweenness remains, and yet I feel at home here.

In Florida, the suburbs were our question. After ten years in the city, we wondered if we could be happy in a house with a garage among the culs-de-sac. The answer seemed to be no, and so our dreams moved in the unforeseen direction of a farmhouse. But since leaving Florida, the suburbs have also been our answer, proving that places always have more potential, and more going on beneath the surface, than our fixed ideas about them. The old Pennsylvania farmhouse we found, with its many small bedrooms for guests, is the fulfillment of our dream, but it's also planted in the suburbs, ringed round with culs-de-sac where Jonathan and I go for long walks and our children play with friends.

Places, like the lives we live in them, are neither fixed nor permanent. Even land can flow, like a river or stream, like the passing of time.

In winter, Lillian, Thaddeus, Beau, and even Elsa sled on golf course hills and ice skate on retention ponds. In spring, our family invites every one of the neighbors to our yard for an Easter egg hunt, and the kids help me fill two thousand plastic eggs with toys and candy. In autumn, we sit together in the backyard nearest to ours and roast marshmallows with neighbors who have become friends. Vision matters so much; without it, the people perish, as one proverb states.[1] Yet even when divinely inspired, our vision is generally hazy and incomplete. It guides us, but its fulfillment contains many surprises. I once found the in-between space of the suburbs unbearable. Now, I am grateful to be making a home in them.

Where is Maplehurst? Perhaps this is the answer to Rand's question: Maplehurst is in between, and it is in process. Places, like the lives we live in them, are neither fixed nor permanent. Even land can flow, like a river or stream, like the passing of time.

If the places we make are meant to be shared, can we share them even while they are in flux? If we plant a tree to hold a hammock or shade a table, what do we do while we wait for that tree to grow? It was a dream of hospitality that led us to Maplehurst. To that end, Maplehurst has been in a process of transformation ever since, and I cannot yet glimpse the end of this journey. It was in Florida, where we struggled to make new friends and felt so distant from all of our old friends, that we began to imagine taking care of some special place where people would want to gather and where we would have room enough for others to come *and* stay. We imagined some young person moving in and sharing family life for a while. We imagined a family in transition who might need a home for a month or more. We imagined the opposite of our insular, independent, and isolated suburban life.

Riding the tide of the country life I envisioned, I brought home an old-fashioned wicker picnic basket from the local thrift store. We packed the basket and took it to the beach one evening. It turned out it wasn't really meant for beach picnics. Our bright blue ice chest on wheels was better suited for that. When I packed the basket with sandwiches and cloth napkins and the straw-berries we had bought from a stand on the side of the highway, I dreamed of filling the basket with the help of guests, stepping outside while a screen door slapped at our heels, and searching, blanket in hand, for just the right shady spot for a picnic.

Simple food and drink may be the only absolutely necessary components of hospitality. I can welcome others even when there is a hole in the front porch where rain has rotted the boards. I can welcome others while scaffolding climbs the brick walls, as it does now that Bill has begun his work here at Maplehurst. I can even welcome others without air conditioning, trusting heaven for a breeze. The welcome we extended to Nara and her children turned out to be a welcome that rebounded back to us. With Nara's encouragement and invigorated by her enthusiasm, I drove miles in search of the best farm stands and grower's markets. Her daughters picked green beans from the raised beds Jonathan had built in the spring, and her son shucked corn in happy, messy confusion on the small porch near the back kitchen door. Together, Beau, Thaddeus, and Josh shredded our entire set of badminton racquets, enthusiastically swatting the harmless bugs with the terrifying name "cicada killers." Nara and her children told us stories of perfect, jewel-like fruit sold in Tokyo's specialty gift shops, but they also told us that the price of corn on the cob meant they were used to cutting each cob into three servings. The large bowl of fresh corn Jonathan had just pulled from our grill suddenly looked to us like what it was: abundance and blessing and one of the sweetest gifts of this place. Through these friends, I was able to see our home with new eyes, with fresh gratitude.

I believe the meals we shared together during that memorable week tasted so good and persist in my memory not despite the serious limitations we were dealing with but because of them. Though both Nara and I often served foods to guests and our other children that our sons could not eat, for this one week we promised to make only meals and snacks everyone could enjoy. This meant we prepared everything without wheat, without dairy, without eggs, without peanuts or tree nuts, and without sesame. We packed that picnic basket with lunches, but instead of sandwiches we stuffed nori and rice with all kinds of fillings: avocado for creaminess, my homemade cucumber pickles for tartness, farmer's market carrots and cucumbers for crunch. We ate picnics of fried chicken, but we fried it the Japanese way: in potato starch and coconut oil. We picked small yellow squash from the garden—squash my children had always refused to eat—and sliced it into ribbons before stirring it into the batter of thin, savory Korean pancakes. Nara even taught me how to make corn tortillas from scratch, and the intense, fresh-corn flavor made everything we folded inside them taste outstanding.

The culmination of our week together arrived on Friday evening. Josh had never eaten pizza before, but in Pennsylvania we had discovered a dedicated gluten-free bakery only ten minutes from our house that sold frozen pizza crusts to go. On our last night together, we spread those crusts with homemade tomato sauce, crumbled sausage from a local farm, and rosemary from the pot outside the kitchen door. Some we dotted with fresh mozzarella, and two we reserved for vegan cheese. Josh and Thaddeus broke bread together with huge smiles while Nara and I took pictures and promised we'd do it again next year. By the time we dropped off our friends at the Philadelphia airport, I felt more settled in both my new home and my new life than I had since arriving a year earlier. It seems we come home, in part, by giving our home away, even if that home is unfinished. And bread that is shared, even if it is gluten-free, satisfies our deepest hunger.

Novelists are placemakers, too, and one of my favorite writers is the man who made a place called Narnia. As a child, one of the things I loved most about that fantasy world was how C. S. Lewis acknowledged hunger and celebrated the goodness of food, a goodness all children know well and feel deeply. Lucy's friendship with Tumnus was cemented while they shared buttered toast and tea. The Pevensies' frightful introduction to Narnia was tempered by a meal of fried trout, buttered potatoes, and a "great and gloriously sticky marmalade roll" prepared by the Beavers.[2] But Lewis also acknowledged that the good gift of food can be twisted and marred. Edmund ate sickly-sweet Turkish Delight with the White Witch, but it was food that would intensify hunger without ever satisfying it. Most memorable for me of all the Narnian meals described by Lewis is the feast of Aslan that occurs after the defeat of the Telmarines in *Prince Caspian*. I have always remembered how the feast began with the trees dancing in slow circles, dropping pieces of themselves that would become a blazing, celebratory bonfire. While Lucy and her Narnian friends enjoyed roasted meat, wheaten cakes and oaten cakes, honey, cream, and fruit, the trees themselves were served by digging moles who brought them rich loam like chocolate and fine gravel "powdered with choice silver sand."[3]

What is true of trees in Narnia, is also true of trees in our world. Trees hunger, but they gratify their hunger in place. For almost every tree, the best food is the crumbly, rich soil of an old forest. The earth itself feeds them, and they are well only to the extent that the soil beneath them is also well. How different, really, is our own hunger? Can we, in Pennsylvania, be nourished by strawberries trucked over miles in plastic clamshell containers just as well as strawberries we grew ourselves or plucked from a farm market table a few miles down the road? This isn't only a question for those preoccupied with food politics, ethics, or dietary rules. And even though the question is complicated by inequalities of income and privilege and even geographic access, it is still a question worth asking. A straightforward but often overlooked fact of life is that places themselves can nourish us and care for us in surprising ways if we will let them. Why not let them?

These days, most of us are so accustomed to an estrangement between our hunger and our home that we do not even notice it, yet this separation is a fairly recent historical development. My father, growing up on a family farm in Comanche County in the 1950s, did not know it. He drank milk from a cow in the backyard barn. He ate fish he'd caught himself. My ancestors, so hungry for land of their own that they wandered all the way to Indian Territory in Texas, did not know it. They needed land to feed their children, and they went in search of it. The violent conflicts between American settlers and those who already called the Great Plains home, like the Comanche, weren't merely confrontations over ownership and land rights. They were conflicts between two very different ways of being sustained by the land, one nomadic, determined by the growth of grass and the movements of the buffalo, and the other more agricultural, rooted in barbed wire and the plow.

The larger story of westward expansion by colonists and pioneers across North America, of which my family history is only a small part, is a story fueled by hunger. We typically imagine that the hunger for a farm of one's own was satisfied through land clearing, tree felling, stump pulling, and general deforestation, but the actual history of how the land was changed is more complex, more interesting, and more flavorful. The early colonists and later pioneers did clear forests for agriculture, but one of the most important ways they lay claim to the land was by planting trees. When George Washington leased portions of his own property holdings, the lease specified: "[W]ithin three years there shall be planted an orchard of 100 apple trees . . . and 100 peach trees, the same to be kept always during the continuance of said lease well pruned, fenced in and secured from horses, cattle and other creatures that might hurt them."[4] When the Ohio Company began developing land in the newly claimed Northwest Territory, they required settlers to plant at least fifty apple trees and twenty peach trees within three years on each one-hundred-acre lot.[5] For land in transition, orchard-planting was agreed to be the surest sign of ownership and a guarantee of legal title. We may be less inclined today to view fallen trees as a sign of progress, but those early settlers at least understood that the ground beneath their feet could feed them if they tended it. Our treeless, chemical-fed lawns seem like a pointless regression compared with apple orchards that gave fruit and cider every autumn.

One of the legendary placemakers in this history of westward expansion from New England, across Pennsylvania, and into the modern states of Ohio, Indiana, Illinois, Michigan, and Wisconsin is John Chapman, a man remembered as a friend to pioneers and Native Americans. Known to us as Johnny Appleseed, his story has been handed down in Disney-esque cartoon colors, but the real man crisscrossed a harsh frontier with sacks of apple seeds fueled by a complicated but inspiring religious fervor. A member of the Christian sect known as Swedenborgianism, Chapman believed the natural world had spiritual value and that nature would persist in the world to come. There was money to be made in planting apple tree nurseries to supply settlers with the trees they would need to feed their pigs, make their cider, and lay claim to land, but Chapman's simple, even ascetic life testifies to a deeper, more spiritual motivation that his contemporaries sought to probe through stories and legends.

One oft-repeated tale is of Chapman sleeping one night in the branches of an oak tree, dreaming he had found a way to plant apple trees straight across the continent from one ocean to another. Chapman himself claimed that "angels told him to be a messenger of peace and to grace the way to the west with an offering of fruit."[6] Chapman planted orchards and gave and sold his trees, and in the process, prepared a path that pioneering families, desperate for land to feed themselves, could follow. Meanwhile, settlers carried his seedlings with them along an Oregon Trail Chapman himself would never travel. Chapman understood physical hunger and spiritual hunger, and he believed his apple trees could temper both. Thousands of square miles were in the process of being remade, but Chapman's infant trees were a peace offering during an often harsh and violent period of our history.

Halfway between our friend Nara's first summer visit and her second, Elsa's babysitter, Julie, mentioned she was looking for an apartment. I had to bite my tongue from immediately inviting her to move into one of the three bedrooms on the third floor. I knew Jonathan would love the idea, but I worried Julie might doubt the invitation if it seemed too spontaneous. What I later tried to explain as we helped her move her belongings into the middle bedroom on the third floor was that this arrangement was neither a surprise nor an imposition. It was the fulfillment of one more aspect of our dream for this place. When our Tokyo friends next came to visit or when family came to stay, Julie would always ask if she was in the way. But when it came to hospitality, she was far less "in the way" than my own kids, especially the younger ones, who are often most in the way when they try to help and who have no shame about squabbling at the table in front of guests. Because Julie lives with us and isn't only a visitor, she sees us, perhaps not at our very worst, but not always at our best either. And yet her presence helps draw out the best in us. With Julie at my table, I am ever so slightly more patient, and the children are at least a little less likely to shout at one another over the last slice of bread. Maplehurst feels even more like the home we've always wanted when Julie is at our dinner table, sharing salmon cakes pan-fried in olive oil and broccoli roasted till it's turned brown and sweet. And I can always count on her not to whine for dessert, unlike a few others at my table.

We may still be waiting for the perfection of "that day," but we prepare for its coming and taste its arrival when we share the places we are making with others or when we receive the hospitality others offer to us.

If home at its best offers deep and abiding peace, then perhaps we are most aware of that gift, with its sense of wholeness and completeness, when we are seated with friends in the shade of a tree. "In that day," the Lord has said, "each of you will invite your neighbor to sit under your vine and fig tree."[7] We may still be waiting for the perfection of "that day," but we prepare for its coming and taste its arrival when we share the places we are making with others or when we receive the hospitality others offer to us. If we waited till we saved up enough for air conditioning, if we waited for Bill to finish repairing the brick walls, if we waited till our children were less in the way or our energy levels less depleted, we would lose out on that glimpse, that foretaste, that reflection of the long-desired day when God's coming kingdom has fully come. We might forget that life's sweetest moments are not so far off, nor so difficult to achieve. We might not realize they are near at hand and as effortless as harvesting the bounty of tomatoes or apples someone else has grown for us.

Chapter 11

Rainbow Eucalyptus and Roses

A PLACE FOR THOSE WHO MOURN

We do the work of heaven when we bring order to the world around us. We are all gardeners of a sort, and most of our lives are dedicated to tending, keeping, and making. We are what author Andy Crouch describes as "creative cultivators," invited to participate in the victory over chaos celebrated in the first chapters of Genesis.[1] Knowing all this, I still hesitated over the decision to make space for a formal flower garden. Though I had always tucked sunny marigolds and nasturtiums in and around the vegetable garden on the eastern side of the house, telling myself that they attract the pollinators my tomatoes and cucumbers need, only the pressure of shifting seasons finally moved me to action. Fall came around again, and I knew if I did not smother the grass with cardboard and compost this winter, I would either need to wait one more year or dig out the sod by hand. I didn't like the thought of either option.

On a freezing cold day, Jonathan and I marked out a forty-by-forty-foot square. We smothered the grass with the flattened cardboard boxes we had saved as well as quite a few more we had collected from the neighborhood sidewalks on recycling day. We spread steaming, black mushroom compost, a cheap but fertile byproduct of our local mushroom farms, in a lumpy layer over the cardboard. In January and February, while the grass beneath the cardboard decomposed, I ordered flowers: bare-root roses, lily bulbs, dahlia tubers, and seed packets of zinnias, cosmos, laceflowers, snapdragons, and black-eyed Susan vine. I waited for spring with only a steaming pile of compost and a basket of seed packets for solace. Yet I felt a growing sense of anticipation, as if I had finally cracked open some essential door.

We are all gardeners of a sort, and most of our lives are dedicated to tending, keeping, and making.

She kept mentioning the rainbow trees, but I never could quite picture them. I don't think I even looked them up in one of my tree books. Instead, I listened to my sister's stories of rainbow-striped bark as if she were telling me about life on Mars—fascinating but irrelevant and too far away to be real. My younger sister Kelli visited Maplehurst only twice (first in autumn, then in spring) before she moved to Hawaii with her husband Shawn and their four children, their youngest having been born less than a year after Elsa. Kelli and I had climbed the mulberry tree in our Texas backyard together as girls, yet she had woken up to the presence and importance of trees years before me. I can remember how I smiled, uncomprehending, when she came to visit us in Chicago, seething about the so-called "crape murder" perpetrated on the crape myrtles in her North Carolina neighborhood. "They whack off the top with pruning saws! It's horrible! Why do they do it?" At the time, I only vaguely knew what a crape myrtle tree looked like, and I couldn't answer her. I couldn't share her outrage.

Eucalyptus deglupta. The rainbow eucalyptus tree. It grows in rainy, tropical forests and regularly sheds its bark in long strips, revealing the brilliant green inner bark. Over time, this green bark matures and changes color, leaving the soaring tree lined with vertical streaks of red, orange, green, blue, and gray. I've since seen these astonishing trees for myself, and I understand why my sister could talk of little else. But what I wanted then was help with another kind of rainbow: what flower varieties should I plant in the new garden? How should I arrange them? What colors should I choose? When I could lead her away from talk of rainbow trees and coconut palms, Kelli's comments about her own flower tending were sobering. "I never did manage to grow a lily," she told me. "Even though we owned a dog, the rabbits ate every single one."

"What about roses?" I asked.

"You'll have to ask Dad about roses. Do you remember how he'd drive us kids the half-hour to the Antique Rose Emporium?"

Unfortunately, I didn't remember. I vaguely recalled a gift shop that sold packets of Texas wildflower seeds such as bluebonnets, but either we had never visited when the roses were in bloom, or I had been blind to flowers I took for granted. The Antique Rose Emporium, a national mecca for lovers of Old Garden Roses, lay halfway between our childhood home and the small town of Brenham, Texas, famous for the Blue Bell Creameries factory. Back then I was more interested in free ice cream samples than roses, though our father had filled the front yard of our Texas home with flowers (he had also filled our freezer with Blue Bell ice cream). I can't recall any of my father's flowers in detail, but I've never forgotten the quarter-sized welts mosquitos left on my face and arms whenever my mother sent me out with scissors to cut roses for the table. I learned to cut roses quickly and precisely.

The same year Kelli was learning how to harvest mangoes from a tree in her Hawaiian backyard (and discovering that the skin of these fruits emits the same potent oil as poison ivy and can cause a similarly potent rash), I was reading everything I could about roses. I had begun in order to choose a few roses for the new garden, but I kept on reading when I discovered a riveting tale of rescue from near extinction. Old Garden Roses, the heirloom varieties France's Empress Josephine may have collected in her famous garden at Château Malmaison, or the white rose of York remembered in the history of England's Wars of the Roses, do not sit in warehouses waiting to be chosen from catalogs. If gardeners stop growing them, they are lost. Sometimes forever. That is what happened when thousands of old rose varieties with names such as 'Marchioness of Lorne' and 'Ile de France' were crowded out of rose catalogs by modern hybrid tea roses called 'Razzle Dazzle' and 'Voodoo.' My copy of Thomas Christopher's book *In Search of Lost Roses* features a painting of fat, pink cabbage roses on its pretty cover, but the story beyond the cover is the tale of how such old-fashioned beauties were preserved only in faded art and tenuous memory.[2] In the 1970s and '80s, some of these roses were rediscovered by self-taught "rose rustlers" who tracked them down, bush by bush, in ghost towns and graveyards. Eager to meet these rustlers and hear their stories, Christopher writes about his trip to a small Texas town called Bryan. Bryan, Texas. My childhood hometown. The very place where I once gathered roses in my father's garden.

My father had purchased quite a few of his roses from the Antique Rose Emporium in Independence, Texas. I asked him recently if he could recall any of their names. He said at first that he could not, that he remembered where he had planted them but not their names. Then, a few hours later, a long list arrived in my email inbox: 'Lady Banks,' a famous yellow climber; 'Mrs. Pierre S. du Pont,' developed in West Grove, Pennsylvania, and named for Alice du Pont of Longwood; a pretty pink survivor rose that would later be identified as 'Old Blush China'; 'Cecile Brunner,' also called the 'Sweetheart Rose'; and 'American Beauty,' a strongly scented, deep-pink climber. My father's list continued for line after line. Sadly, the roses he had planted were promptly ripped out by the new owners of our Texas house when he and my mother moved to Kansas, but they had persisted in his memory more than even he had been aware.

The astonishing story of antique roses is a story of persistence on every level: the persistence of the plants themselves and the persistence of those who searched for them and found them. The Antique Rose Emporium was established when a central Texas nursery owner in search of native plants stumbled upon an enormous rambling rose growing on a neglected chain-link fence. That rose was later identified as 'Mermaid.' Described as "remarkably vigorous" and "wickedly thorny," 'Mermaid' has creamy, yellow flowers as big as teacup saucers and grows to fifteen or twenty feet.[3] In warmer climates it is a good choice for hiding ugly outbuildings or burying unsightly fences. But despite this plant's beauty and utility, the Texas plantsman discovered that 'Mermaid' was no longer offered for sale by any-one, anywhere. The cuttings he collected from that forgotten rose launched his emporium, a thriving and internationally rec-ognized business preserving old roses through commerce. The antique varieties rediscovered and reintroduced by the Antique Rose Emporium are now known as "survivor roses." Many of these survivors were first introduced to American gardens by rose growers from a small Pennsylvania town known as "Home of the Roses."[4] I found that old nickname in a postcard history book of West Grove, Pennsylvania. West Grove. The little vil-lage near Maplehurst. The hometown of my choosing.

I was raised by a rose-growing father in Bryan, Texas, the hometown of so many famous "rose rustlers." I have come home to West Grove, Pennsylvania, "Home of the Roses." How could I have worried for so long about cultivating a flower garden? When we first came to Maplehurst, I had only the vaguest idea that commercial nurseries once dominated the local economy until the night I sat up in bed reading *Onward and Upward in the Garden* by Katharine White. White's creative efforts are not as well-known as the books penned by her famous husband, E. B. White, but *Onward and Upward* is as much a classic of garden writing as *Charlotte's Web* is a classic of children's literature. In a chapter on "the changing rose," she writes with longing of West Grove, Pennsylvania's "gently rolling farmland" planted "in long, contoured rows of young roses."[5] "I have never been there," she writes, "but thousands make the pilgrimage" to view a "living catalogue" of new roses each September.

Later, I would learn that even Mark Hughes was a partner in one of the largest local nursery businesses before he built Maplehurst and began to raise Guernsey cattle. Today, that same business is called "Star Roses". It is still headquartered in West

Grove, and it is responsible for the famous 'Knock Out' family of roses that have become the most widely sold rose in North America. But rose lovers no longer make a pilgrimage to this village. The east coast display gardens have closed, the growing fields relocated to more favorable climates in California and Arizona, and most of my neighbors, when I have mentioned the local importance of the rose, have never heard the stories and have no idea why our local streets are named for roses, trees, and Guernsey cattle.

Despite the romantic histories and evocative names, it isn't easy to spend money and have only flowers to show for it. It isn't like a donation to a charity. It isn't like a deposit in a savings account. A flower isn't even a carrot. I cannot fill my stew pot with flowers. That first winter, the balance on our bank statement dwindled with the purchase of each bare-root rose and lily bulb, yet I did not have even flowers to show for it. The view from the parlor window remained the same: bleak and brown. Dreams ask for commitment. They require a running leap. They require patient waiting. Jonathan and I had smothered the lawn, and there could be no going back. In a month or two, cardboard boxes labeled "fragile," "this side up," and "live plants" would begin showing up on the porch near the back door. I looked forward to planting antique roses with names like 'Souvenir de la Malmaison,' 'Sombreuil,' and 'Madame Hardy,' a white rose with a stunning green button-eye that I had ordered from the Antique Rose Emporium. And still I wondered. *Even if this flower garden dream is one day realized, even if the roses take root and grow, will Jonathan and I say it was worthwhile?*

Spring arrives in the garden long before it arrives anywhere else. As soon as the last snow melted, as soon as the muck began to thaw, we were out in it. Jonathan built, slowly, picket by picket, a fence. Together we marked the paths with twine and a few well-placed stakes. The air was still cold enough to make me wish for fleece-lined gardening gloves, but with freezing hands I buried lily bulbs and the woody bare roots of roses along the edges of the still-theoretical paths. I hoped our measurements would prove true. I hoped they would prove *us* true. I tended seedlings in the basement. Zinnias, in white and salmon-pink, cosmos, sweet-scented alyssum, and laceflowers stretched beneath the faux sunlight of fluorescent shop lights. My gardening books talk of plant combinations and color palettes, but designing a garden is all so much more uncertain than paint on a canvas or words on a page. With the help of my sister, my father, and many books, I chose my varieties with care, but I could not know then that the newly amended soil would be too fertile for cosmos and laceflowers—the cosmos would grow into feathery green monsters but never bloom, and the laceflowers would leap and flower but quickly rot away. I could not know that the salmon-pink zinnias would turn out to be more of a garish orange. I could not know that the white zinnias would glow in the evening like moonlight and starlight and magic.

Dreams ask for commitment. They require a running leap. They require patient waiting.

We hosted an Easter egg hunt for our neighbors, as we had done every year since our first spring at Maplehurst. Nothing yet grew in the garden except candy-filled eggs and tiny green boxwood shrubs. Paths were merely the suggestion of rain-sodden string. "What is that?" my neighbors asked, pointing toward the great brown square. "What are you doing?"

"Dreaming," I did not answer them. "Hoping," I did not say.

"That's our new flower garden!" I explained with a hearty voice and a trembling smile.

Jonathan and I consoled ourselves with every gardener's favorite refrain: *Next year. Next year, won't this be the perfect spot for an Easter egg hunt? Next year, won't the roses be beautiful? Next year, won't we say how glad we are to have done this?*

The wild thing about next year is that it always does come. And so much more quickly than we ever dare to hope. When you tend gardens and young children, this is both a marvelous and a heartbreaking thing. We hosted another Easter egg hunt for our neighbors this spring. This year, toddlers crunched across the garden's gravel paths scooping up eggs. The window boxes in the potting shed spilled the old-fashioned violets called "Johnny Jump-Ups," in purple, gold, and white. The green boxwoods edged beds that, while still mostly brown and mostly empty, at least looked like what they were: places where flowers would soon grow.

Next year gives and it takes away, but what it gives and what it takes are so often unexpected.

Next year gives and it takes away, but what it gives and what it takes are so often unexpected. This year gave perfectly formed daffodils despite our strangely warm El Niño winter. This year took the life of Kelli's husband Shawn in a military helicopter crash off the beautiful blue coast of Oahu. In January, before spring, before the egg hunt with neighbors, I flew with twelve-year-old Lillian to Hawaii. When we boarded the plane, we still hoped that Shawn was not dead but lost. We imagined what was never true: twelve marines, together, on a life raft. Twelve men heading home from the sea.

I first saw the rainbow trees as we drove from the little island town of Kailua toward the formidable waves of the North Shore. Kelli and Shawn had made their home two blocks from Kailua's friendly beach in a neighborhood of palm trees and colorful bungalows, but the drive north revealed an otherworldly landscape where jagged green mountains guarded agricultural fields red with volcanic soil. As we drove, the rainbow trees were on my right, more strange and bright than I had imagined. On my left were the pineapple fields of the Dole plantation. Flashing past our car window were rows of spiky, low-growing plants, each endowed with a green pineapple crown. So far, everything I'd experienced of Hawaii was like those sharp pineapple leaves: fierce and beautiful but so unfamiliar, so unlike the home I knew and loved, that I could not imagine how anyone could feel at home in this place. Rainbows, enormous and ever-present. Sharp, vertical cliffs and dripping waterfalls, their edges barely softened by green velvet growth. Crashing waves, so wild and loud they deserved the name *chaos*, the same name the ancients had given the sea. This terrible ocean had taken Shawn from us, and in the days of the rescue operation, when we had begged for calm seas, this ocean had defied us. It seemed to me the farthest thing from home because it was unknown, unloved, and uncontrollable.

Had that chaos taken Shawn? Would Kelli and their kids be left holding only sorrow and confusion? Shawn left for work one day and never came home, and his well-worn boots were still sitting by the back door of his Kailua house. His shirts were still in the basket near the washing machine. But where had he gone? And where were we without him? So many men and women, by air and by sea, had searched for him and his companions in the waters. But that first day and that second night following the accident, the winter waves of the North Shore writhed and thrashed to heights that astonished even the locals. It was as if all creation groaned with us, yet Shawn was not waiting for rescue. A life raft was found, but it was empty. It had always been empty.

That evening when I first saw the rainbow trees, having driven to the far side of the pineapple fields, I finally stood on North Shore sand alongside my parents and a small group of local residents. I thought I was positioned well back from those treacherous waves, but their pattern, if they followed one, was devious. One wave unexpectedly crashed far above the others, and my long sundress was suddenly soaked to the knees. The older man at my side stepped neatly back from the water and said, "Right there, about two miles out. That's where I saw the bright light. That's where the marines went down." I said nothing, only stared where he had pointed. This man had been introduced to me as "a famous old surfer" by Don, the owner of this North Shore home and the friend of a family I had attended church with as a girl. This famous man's name meant nothing to me, but when he began to talk, his voice was soft and had the cadence of water lapping at the shore. I listened to him tell story after story about waves—Hawaii waves and Florida waves and even New Jersey waves—and we laughed together while the sun sank. When our faces were lost in the darkness and only our voices remained, he told me, as if he'd been aiming for these words all along, "If I could choose where to die, I would choose this place. These waves. This water. Right about there." And he pointed again toward the horizon and that spot where, just a few nights before, a bright light and a terrible sound had shaken his world and ours.

The waves that looked like chaos to me—unknown, unloved, untameable—looked like home to him. "When I'm standing here on the edge," he said, "I only want to be back, out there, in the waves." And I pictured him then, at rest on his board, the curl of a blue wave like a roof overhead. I loved silver trees. He loved salty waves. We looked at both through eyes of love, which means, I think, that we each saw what God sees.

The waves were not chaos. They were created, they were known, like every rainbow tree, every palm tree, and every maple tree. The ancient words from Isaiah, words we'd been repeating to one another for days, were true: "When you pass through the waters, I will be with you."[6] Shawn was not lost to chaos. We were not left with confusion. A door had opened. He had walked through. And this door had appeared for Shawn in one of the most beautiful places on the planet, a place where rainbows embrace the whole horizon, a place where sea turtles swim and whales sing songs. That night, I underlined the words of the psalmist: "The waters saw you, God, the waters saw you and writhed; the very depths were convulsed . . . Your path led through the sea, your way through the mighty waters, though your footprints were not seen."[7]

One of the most storied roses in the world is a hybrid tea rose whose petals are pale yellow blushed with pink. It is so well known, most of my rose books do not bother describing it, but those that do call it simply, "the most famous rose of all time."[8] It is undoubtedly a beautiful rose, but it owes much of its fame to two things: the timing of its birth and the name that was given to it. Developed in France during the late 1930s, the rose was smuggled out of occupied France and introduced to American buyers by West Grove's own Conard-Pyle Company. In France, it had been given the name 'Madam A. Meilland,' but in West Grove, Pennsylvania, it was rechristened and reintroduced to a world unmade by war. By luck, by coincidence, or by something else we can't quite name, the date long-planned for the launch of the rose was April 29, 1945—the very same day the Soviet army crossed the Moltke bridge, ensuring the fall of Berlin. The new rose was given the name 'Peace.'[9]

The war was over, and post-war gardeners, tired of their victory vegetables, planted Peace roses everywhere they could. When delegates from forty-nine countries met to form the United Nations, each head of delegation was given a single Peace rose and a note that read, "We hope that the 'Peace' rose will influence men's thoughts for everlasting world peace."[10] Millions of Peace roses have been planted since the war, and the rose itself has been used to breed hundreds of new varieties. Peace is a beautiful rose and a fruitful rose, but knowing West Grove as I do, I see little of coincidence in its name. This area has been cultivated by Quaker men and women who saw no distinction between peacemaking and placemaking. I am not at all surprised that their peaceful vision continues to be planted in gardens around the world.

> Peace dwells in many places, but it seems to dwell in gardens, in particular.

I recently spent time rereading the entries under "Rosa" in *Dirr's Encyclopedia of Trees and Shrubs*. I wondered if Michael Dirr had anything to say about the famous Peace rose, but I found a personal story I didn't remember noticing before. In his introduction, Dirr tells a story about his beloved daughter Susy, his youngest child. Susy carried the gene for cystic fibrosis and received two double-lung transplants. In order to better care for their daughter, Dirr and his wife, Bonnie, sold their home with its well-established garden and began a new garden at a house near their daughter's hospital. Susy died ten years ago, only three years before the publication of this monumental book that has guided me, inspired me, and entertained me. Following Susy's death, the Dirrs moved again, and immediately began digging in yet another garden. "Books are written on dealing with grief," Dirr writes, "but Bonnie and I find inner peace . . . in the garden."[11]

I am more skilled at book-making than garden-making. In the garden, my enthusiasm far exceeds my knowledge. But I agree wholeheartedly with Dirr, and his single sentence speaks as power- fully as any book. Peace dwells in many places, but it seems to dwell in gardens, in particular. Gardens are not as perfect as nature. They are not as grand or

> *Gardens are a place of encounter with the God who draws near. In a garden, we find Christ, who is our peace.*

majestic. They reveal our all-too-human mistakes as readily as our accomplishments. But they are also more hospitable. Unlike a forest, they grow on a human scale. Gardens are a place of encounter with the God who draws near. In a garden, we find Christ, who is our peace.

In April, we buried Shawn in Texas prairie soil. In June, I snipped roses and gathered the first lilies with Shawn's children, my two nieces and my two nephews. Every day of her visit at Maplehurst, my youngest niece helped me fill a collection of buckets with weeds. We fed the weeds, one by one, to the chickens. "These eggs will be full of vitamins!" we took turns saying to one another. Of course, a flower garden costs so much more than a carton of free-range eggs from the market. There is the money for bare roots and bulbs. There is the time spent pruning and weeding.

There is the frustration of watching Japanese beetles devour rose buds from the inside out. One moment it is Eden, and the next a sudden rainstorm has flattened half of the trumpet lilies. When I count the costs, I begin to doubt. But when I remember my sister taking photographs of the roses in delicate rainbow colors, when I think of my niece pulling green velvetweeds, I say, "How glad I am to have made this garden."

Placemakers make large places, and we make small ones, and there are quite a few smaller places within this larger place I call home. There is the squishy sofa in the small sunroom, a good place to sit with a book. There is the bench shaded by wild grape vines halfway down the driveway, a good place to hide. There is the fenced-in square of the vegetable garden, a good place for sneaking the first ripe cherry tomatoes, quickly, into your mouth. But this summer, the place I love most is the flower garden. With an Amish-made shed for shelter, two benches for rest, and a wild abundance of blooms, the flower garden has grown into a sanctuary. It is a place where peace dwells, the kind of peace that persists regardless of grief or thunderstorms or insects. We made it with our own hands, yet it feels like a gift I did nothing to deserve. Whether I am picking weeds, or squashing beetles, or cutting a frilly pink dahlia the exact size of young Elsa's head, I keep looking for someone to acknowledge. Of course, a sanctuary is also a good place for prayer. Perhaps that is why, as I work, I do not whistle. I only whisper, *Thank you.*

In October, we planted a tree for Shawn. I had first considered planting a rose, but I wanted to give Kelli and her kids a special place here at Maplehurst where they could remember Shawn and feel near to him, and no plant creates places the way a tree creates places. What I wanted more than anything was to give them peace, and I have always felt most at peace in the shade of a spreading tree. On their first Father's Day without their dad, Shawn's kids helped me choose a tree from a nursery catalog. We settled on a northern red oak, *Quercus rubra*. The pictures made it seem handsome and strong, like a white oak, but with the added bonus of brilliant fall color. Long after we ordered it, I learned that this tree is also known as a champion oak, and it has been called "one of the biggest, stateliest, and handsomest trees of eastern North America."[12] The Arbor Day Foundation says, "it is widely considered a national treasure."[13] I scheduled delivery for fall planting, but September went and October marched on, and I still had not heard anything from the nursery about our tree.

Just before October turned over into November, at that time of year when the church remembers all saints and all souls, my brother-in-law, Brian, traveled with his son Josiah to spend a few days at Maplehurst. Brian is married to Lisa, my youngest sister, and Josiah is near in age to Beau. Brian planned to run the Marine Corps marathon in Washington D.C. in honor of Shawn, but he would spend a few days before and after the race with us and with my brother, Nathan, and his wife, Amanda. Nathan and Amanda left their older three children with friends in Texas and flew up with their youngest, a baby boy who had been born while our family gathered in Hawaii in the days after Shawn's death. We had received the message about his birth just as we stepped into the hangar for the Marine Corps' official memorial service. In that moment, as we stood in a huddle looking at a photo of a tiny infant on Kelli's phone, death was turned inside out. A baby boy had entered this breathing world, and he shared his middle name, Matthew, with Shawn.

The day before the marathon, I picked up a message on our voicemail. Apparently there had been some mistake or confusion, and the nursery had failed to notify us that our tree had been ready to be picked up for weeks. "It's right here," a kind voice assured me. "We've been taking good care of it. Maybe you'd like to bring it home today?" And that is how Shawn's oak tree came to be planted by all three of his brothers on Kelli's side of the family: one brother who lives on the West Coast, one who lives on the East Coast, and one who calls the far South home. Jonathan brought the tree back in the bed of our pickup truck. Brian pulled it in a wheeled cart down the length of our driveway. Nathan steadied it with his hand. We chose a high spot with plenty of space and sun, and Nathan, Brian, and Jonathan, one Day son and the men who married two Day daughters, took turns digging a hole. My own children were at school, but I gave Josiah the watering can, and he watered his Uncle Shawn's tree well. Beau and I may have failed in our acorn-planting efforts, but I no longer minded. Maplehurst has its oak tree now, and a little boy watered it while I whispered a prayer of blessing: *May you grow tall, may you grow deep. May Shawn's children always find peace in your shade.*

Chapter 12

Arboretum

THE PLACE WHERE WE
CULTIVATE PEACE

Great trees have a hold on the earth we cannot match. They stretch and grow and renew their leaves over such a long time, they fit in their place in the earth—belong to it—in ways we may dream of belonging but never entirely achieve. Unlike the long-lived white oak that still dances in place on the edge of the golf course, we are not rooted. We roam, and we wander. Much like the flowers or grass in the field, our lives are fleeting. Sometimes I am glad about this. I have no desire to live so long that I become hollowed out like a silver maple. And I am glad my eyes have seen the rainbow trees on a faraway island in a faraway sea. But I have always longed for roots, and I have always wanted to belong to some particular place. To grow roots, we must choose at times to be still, to dance in place. I have learned that lesson from the trees.

While some trees submit to transplantation more readily

than others, no tree loves to have its roots disturbed. White oak trees, with their long, embedded taproot, are especially problematic to move. Michael Dirr says they are "quite difficult to transplant" and should only be relocated "as a small tree, ideally of less than 2 1/2-inch caliper, for best success."[1] I once read a story about a private tree sanctuary in the Pacific Northwest. There is a man there who digs out and replants healthy trees that would otherwise be cut down and discarded for various reasons. He loves his trees and knows the story of each one, but it grieves him to admit that despite his knowledge and despite his care, only 60 percent of his trees survive being moved.[2]

To grow roots, we must choose at times to be still, to dance in place.

For eight years, I have chosen to stay away from our old home in Chicago, as if my new life could be firmly established only if I did not uproot myself in order revisit the past. I've had a few layovers at Chicago's airports, but a view of gray clouds and brown bungalows from 10,000 feet is not a real return. Once, my friend Melissa and I flew from Philadelphia to Chicago for a reunion with Aimee and Jessica. Aimee picked us up at Midway Airport, but she drove straight north to our Wisconsin vacation rental. I did not ask if she would detour east through Hyde Park, and I probably would have said, *No, thank you*, even if she had offered. I have worried that the past might have the power to destabilize the future we are trying to make at Maplehurst. My roots have now sunk more than five years deep in Pennsylvania soil. I hope that is deep enough, because it feels as if a current is drawing me back to that great lake, and a wind is lifting me toward honey locust trees.

A few years ago, I sat with Rand and Aimee around the kitchen table at Maplehurst, and I promised to revisit Hyde Park for our church's twentieth anniversary celebration. January may not have been the most auspicious month for the birth of a new neighborhood church in Chicago, but that little church took root, grew, and prospered, though it had been planted in a season when even regular churchgoing people would be forgiven for staying indoors on a Sunday morning. Now, twenty years have passed since the founding of the Hyde Park church community that once meant so much to Jonathan and me. My airfare is purchased, and my hotel is reserved. I am leaving home. *Am I also going home?* There is no easy label for what Chicago still means to me.

Unfortunately, the timing of this return feels more like an interruption than an invitation. Our kids can't miss school this month, so Jonathan will stay with them at Maplehurst. January is probably the cruelest season for travel to Chicago, and even if my flight makes it through without weather delays, that famous Chicago wind chill will still be waiting for me. The book I am writing is due in two weeks. It seems foolish to leave my writing desk with that deadline looming. The book isn't finished because I've been asking questions I do not yet know how to answer. *Is it possible to cultivate places where peace can dwell? If so, does that work endure? Can it bear lasting fruit?* But perhaps I don't really want the answers. Perhaps I'm afraid to return. I'm afraid to see with my own eyes that Jonathan and I left no mark at all in that neighborhood we loved and tended for a decade. I don't want to feel myself a stranger beneath honey locust trees I once knew so well.

Not long after Bill first set up his scaffolding around our house, Jonathan dug out that humiliating letter from our home insurer and made an appointment with our local agent. I worried the whole time he was away. *Will they cancel our policy? Or will they trust our good intentions and our plans?* Jonathan was gone for hours, but he came home with good news. He told me how he had sat with our agent, Debbie, in a back office in a red brick building on West Grove's main street. He passed paperwork and photographs across the desk, and he spoke of Bill and John. Debbie finally interrupted him to say, "As long as we can see you're making progress on the house, you'll be fine. By the way, my own windows are in terrible shape. Who did you say is doing your repairs?" That is how we discovered Debbie also lives in an old red brick house. In fact, hers was the first brick house in town, and it was built by West Grove's founder, a Quaker named Joseph Pyle. Debbie and Jonathan quickly abandoned the subject of insurance in order to talk about old houses—the pleasure and the pain.

Long, long ago, the front porch of the Joseph Pyle house was built at exactly the height of a horse-drawn carriage door. Ladies in full skirts once stepped with ease from carriage to porch, but Debbie explained how that period detail made the porch difficult to repair and impossible to retrofit for compliance with modern building codes. Still, she'd insisted on repairing rather than replacing it, and she'd dug deep in order to pay for the extra time and effort that required. Today, the porch still looks much as it did when Pyle first conceived it. Debbie also told Jonathan about a hidden cupboard in the floor where ladies could store their boots after changing into dancing shoes and about windows that no longer kept out the cold. Finally she said, "Joseph Pyle built a brick kiln here in town. I still have piles of bricks from that kiln in my yard, and they probably match the bricks at Maplehurst. You're welcome to take any you might need." In this way, the awful letter that led us to Bill also led us to a stash of antique bricks Bill could use to rebuild our walls.

Joseph Pyle was a placemaker after Penn's own heart, and when he died in 1909, the headline of his obituary in the local newspaper read, "Well Done, Good And Faithful."[3] Before West Grove began to be developed, Pyle decided, perhaps for reasons of safety and durability, that the new town should consist primarily of brick houses. And so Joseph Pyle built a kiln for manufacturing bricks out of local clay. My hometown is still distinguished by its long main street of "brave brick houses." When I give someone driving directions to Maplehurst, I tell them to exit the highway and turn where the row of solid Victorian brick houses begins.

While reading about this good and faithful man, I came across a description of what this place was like before 1860, the year the railroad arrived and injected the area with the energy of progress. The words first appeared in the inaugural issue of West Grove's own newspaper, published in 1884, when Maplehurst was only about four years old. The passage moves me, and it troubles me, but it helps me see more clearly what I have only before imagined. When the brick houses were still an insubstantial vision in Joseph Pyle's mind, there was already in this place "a grove of gigantic oaks," a "pond of large size," and many "springs of water." This confident reporter insists that only twenty-five years previously, "nature's gifts" ran "to waste" until men saw in the oak trees and abundant water "a rich field for development." The town of West Grove was duly established, and "the marks of nature

> *It strikes me as beautifully poetic that our strongest, safest houses are made of rock and clay, the same "dust" of our own making.*

were supplanted with those of art." But what was the substance of this art? And what was erased from the landscape in order to prepare a clean canvas? Humanity's art looks like "dwellings and storehouses." It sounds like "the stroke of a hammer, the clang of the engine, the rattle of heavy vehicles." It is, according to this West Grove reporter, an art of "animation, energy and enterprise." These things are what took the place of "the mighty oaks upon whose bank crept the delicate and fantastic vine," and the trees had no choice but "to bow their heads in submission to the wants of man."[4] I love the shade of an old oak tree. I love the shelter of a solid brick house. I hope my own creative efforts need never choose between the two.

The creation story of Genesis is unlike the creation myths of other ancient religions because it states that we are made of the same raw material as the world around us. We are not offspring of the gods. We are made of dust. We may bear the image of a creator, but we also share kinship with stars and starfish, with turtles and, yes, with trees. It strikes me as beautifully poetic that our strongest, safest houses are made of rock and clay, the same "dust" of our own making. But more than poetry, there is also, perhaps, a warning, a caution, and a call to humility. We are only dust. Our brave brick houses are also only dust, and even a stone barn can crumble away to almost nothing. A solid brick house is a wonderful thing, worth building and worth restoring. But I long for some form in which nature and art can meet and intermingle. I long for some place where the person who makes bricks and the God who makes trees can meet, face to face. I see now why I love arboretums, those gardens devoted to

I long for some place where the person who makes bricks and the God who makes trees can meet, face to face.

trees. These are middle places. In them, extremes are reconciled. Peace is made.

As my plane heads toward Chicago's Midway Airport, I feel the return of that familiar, despairing question: *Is life anything more than a litany of the things we lost in winter?* I cannot imagine that my old home in Chicago can now be much more to me than a dead end where grief and memory swirl. But the sadness I feel in anticipation of my return is soon rattled by disorientation. There were no hotels in the heart of Hyde Park when I moved away, but my Uber driver drops me off at a shiny, metallic mid-rise hotel. The street corner itself is familiar, but most of the buildings and shops seem stylish and new. I remember how even before our move, I had heard that the university planned to redevelop this commercial strip, but I am unprepared for the way eight years can transform vague talk into solid hotels and bakeries, steamy coffee shops and the most adorable fudge and ice cream store I've ever seen. The only familiar sights are the pizza place across the street (Jonathan and I loved their rosemary and potato pizza) and the movie theater on the corner. That theater closed down years before we moved, but I remember our last visit with our good friends Jesh and Jessica. I can't recall the movie we saw, but I have never forgotten the question we were asked at the ticket booth: "You want heat or no heat?" Apparently the heating system had broken down, and only one screening room was warm. We chose heat. That memory makes me laugh, and I pull out my phone to take a picture of the new, snazzy Harper Theater with its flashing marquee. This, at least, is better than when we left it, and I feel a surge of curiosity. *What else has eight years improved?*

Most of us are used to the idea that places we knew in childhood will seem smaller when we revisit them, but I am surprised to find that these familiar places from my adult life have also changed size over the years of my absence. Our memories may be sharp and clear, but they are never an exact match for the experience of moving our body through physical space. I walk by the church where Lillian and Thaddeus attended preschool, and I see the trio of lilac shrubs they once climbed every afternoon with their school friends. In my memory, those lilacs are as tall as trees, and I have often wondered since what variety of lilac could possibly grow so tall. But I see now that these are ordinary lilacs, perhaps ten feet tall, just like the one near the white picket fence at Maplehurst. How small my children must have been that these lilacs had seemed so large in my memory.

I walk for hours this first afternoon, and I quietly dissolve into tears three times: twice at playgrounds I visited almost daily with my children, and once while standing on the sidewalk across the street from Eaton Place. I know my friend Tracy still lives there, but I don't ring the buzzer. I can't imagine being strong enough to reenter this building. I would be washed away by a tsunami of memory. I want only small memories. Manageable memories. Like the memory of Paul Cornell that comes back to me as I walk south on Cornell Avenue toward the Windermere.

When Mark Hughes was only a little boy growing up on his father's farm near the oak grove that would become West Grove, Paul Cornell, a New England lawyer and entrepreneur, moved to the growing city of Chicago. He was the cousin of Ezra Cornell who founded Cornell University, and he immediately built relationships with Chicago's governing elite. Acting on the advice of Senator Stephen Douglas, Cornell purchased 300 acres of lakefront land south of the city of Chicago. As the city grew, the resort suburb Cornell had named Hyde Park Village was absorbed into Chicago's patchwork of neighborhoods, but the unique qualities Cornell had envisioned and then achieved for the area persisted: homes, businesses, and a university woven together by a beautifully designed park system that prioritized the lakefront, green space, and trees.[5] Cornell's efforts helped realize the vision Chicago city leaders had first planted during the 1830s when they officially gave their city the Latin motto *Urbs in horto*, or "City in a garden."[6]

On the first night of the reunion, I eat dinner with Nara in a dimly lit restaurant that is new to both of us. She flew in from Tokyo only a few days ago. We pry apart mussels in fragrant broth and eat crispy, roasted Brussel sprouts, and we marvel at being together again in Hyde Park. The first gathering of the reunion, a service of celebration, is held just after dinner in a solid, spacious building the church purchased only a year ago. I sit next to Nara beneath the soaring arch of the sanctuary's wooden ceiling and remember all the years we prayed for a church building of our own. I remember the board meetings, the planning, the careful budgets. And though I participated in all those things, I also remember how impossible a building of our own had always seemed to me. O me of little faith. I had sown seeds I never believed would grow, yet God had prospered those seeds despite my doubts and my tendency toward despair.

During a break in the service, I hug my friend Pam for the first time in years. She looks me in the eyes and says, "Your story goes on here. As long as we live here, we'll keep sharing all the seeds of love and compassion that you planted in our hearts so long ago." Her tender words shake me, and I begin to cry again. But these tears are different, and I feel the hard shell of my anxious grief begin to crack and fall away.

After the benediction, I sit for a long while with my friend Meredith, picking up the threads of a friendship that was first established amongst tomatoes and runaway mint in that Woodlawn community garden. It was Meredith who planted the cantaloupe that was stolen just before it reached perfect, tantalizing ripeness. I don't think Meredith was responsible for the mint (I'm fairly certain Joy and I perpetrated that garden crime), but it was our mutual friend Marion (she had settled for a brilliant career in medicine after failing to become a professional gardener) who showed us how to dig it out, pot it up, and then bury the pot back in the ground in order to contain those voracious, spreading roots. Meredith has since moved to an old house in Wisconsin, and we trade restoration stories full of joy and aggravation. She tells me about the raised beds her husband made for their backyard garden, and she says she keeps a framed photograph of our Woodlawn community garden on her wall.

"Have you gone back to that block?" she asks.

"No," I answer. "That garden grows in other places now, doesn't it?"

The weekend moves gently along. I do not feel rushed, though I still haven't found time to catch up with Tracy. On the morning of the day my flight will leave, she calls and asks if I have time to drop by her place before heading to the airport. Here is the invitation to Eaton Place I did not think I wanted, but I have missed Tracy, so I say yes. Leaving my suitcase to pack when I return, I set out from my hotel and begin walking north. Snow has fallen during the night, and the neighborhood has been quietly transformed. Gritty urban streets look like fairytale paths. The bare branches of the honey locust trees have sprouted lacy white leaves.

When I arrive at Eaton Place, I press the button with Tracy's last name on it, and I offer a cheery *Hello!* into the intercom when she answers. She buzzes me in, but I struggle to open the heavy front door. *Is this a new door? Or have I forgotten how the door handle worked?* The weight of eight years falls heavily on me at this thought. Finally, I manage to open it, but I can't make it past the mailboxes and up the second set of steps to the foyer door before Tracy stops pressing the buzzer. I jiggle the second doorknob, but I know this door will be locked. I have been in this same predicament many times, but always I was the one poking my head into the stairwell, trying to determine if my visitor managed to pass through both doors or not. I know if I stand here long enough, Tracy will realize I have not made it through, and she will hit the buzzer again. I stand still, preparing to reenter my past.

The door buzzes again, and I open it. This door, at least, seems to work as it should. I can't decide if the carpet at my feet is the same. The carriage lights above my head are definitely the ones I chose, though smaller than I had remembered. The pale yellow paint we had finally picked out for the walls after many months of debating the idea of wallpaper is less vivid than the color in my memory but otherwise the same. Perhaps I have forgotten the exact shade, or perhaps it has faded over time. I climb the stairs, my hand on the familiar yellow wood of the banister. *I can do this. I am doing this!* But when I reach the third floor, the sight of a boot tray filled with children's shoes outside Tracy's door brings to mind the boot tray that once sat outside our own front door. I can still see Lillian's little red snow boots. Elsa wore them at Maplehurst only a few winters ago. Tracy opens her door, and I turn right instead of the old, familiar left. I hug Tracy with a big smile and tears in my eyes.

Pam said I had sown seeds that were still bearing fruit, but how had I done that? How was it accomplished? I sit at Tracy's dining room table, a cup of hot coffee in my hand, and realize that this, right here, is how it was done. Like Tracy, I opened the door. Hugged. Made coffee. Cleared the table and pulled back a chair. The work may have been spiritual, but it wasn't disembodied. It was dishes washed and candles lit. It was coffee brewed and a soft sofa. It was birthday cake and Thai takeout. It was shared space. It was welcome.

Tracy welcomes me, and we talk of the miracle that brought her family into this building in the first place. We remember how the apartment in the basement suddenly came available for rent, and Jonathan and I, knowing Jim and Tracy needed to move, recommended them to our neighbors as potential tenants. For a while, our kids happily ran up and down four flights of stairs to visit one another, but when Jonathan and I put our apartment on the market in order to move to Florida, the worst possible thing happened: our neighbors across the hall lost their own apartment to foreclosure. We were sad for them and worried for ourselves. How could we sell our place when its mirror across the landing was being offered at a bargain-basement price? In a series of events that still astonishes us eight years later, our apartment sold quickly for the asking price to a couple who have subsequently been good neighbors all these years. And Tracy and her husband were able to buy an apartment just right for a growing family at an almost unbelievable price.

The snow is falling more thickly and more softly as I walk back to my hotel. The flakes are fatter, lacier, and they cling to my eyelashes and slide, only slowly, down my cheeks before resting in the folds of my scarf and around the buttons of my coat. I feel held by this snow, caressed by it, and it suddenly seems that this is the snowfall I have been waiting for ever since that first terrible year in Florida, when I realized I had traded snowflakes for wood ash and smoke. All the snow that has fallen on Maplehurst for six winters has not been enough to heal something in me that desperately needs healing. Maplehurst has her healer now, but I have always had mine. My own healer, my own Maker, brought me back to Chicago, back to gray stone and wrought-iron fence railings softened by snow, back to dear friends and a much-loved apartment home, so that precious memory could become present reality.

Resurrection and eternity are mysteries to me, almost unfathomable, but standing in the snow on a Hyde Park sidewalk, I see an integration of past and present and future that shines like a brilliant, sparkling promise. We believe that a time will come when God will restore everything.[7] The full scope and meaning of that restoration are beyond my understanding, but I finally have an unshakeable hope for broken bricks and fallen trees and every last treasured thing we lost in winter. *Go ahead and love*, I whisper to my heart. *It won't be lost. It won't be wasted.*

Pruned back to its core, this is a book about my longing for peace and my instinct that peace and place are indistinguishable. But it is also a book about God's longing, a longing that weaves in and out and through the whole story the Bible tells. God longs for the place he has chosen as a dwelling for his Name.[8] First there was a garden. Then there was a great land. There was a tribe, a tent, an ark, a temple. There was a city, a Son, and a church.

Today, there is me. Today, there is you. So many homes God has had, and to each one of us, he says, *I am knocking. Please let me in. You are* my *home. I am* your *home. Remain in me.* But remaining is not such an easy thing to do. To remain requires a stillness and a steadfastness in spite of the many things that will make us want to pick up and run. All my life I have been afraid of loss. I have been afraid of goodbyes, of decay, of endings, of death. Loss is painful, sometimes catastrophic, but like some terrible, black soil, it also has the potential to bear exquisite fruit. Childhood memories grow roses. Adult sorrows grow oak trees. Something or someone precious crashes through the canopy of the forest, and there is death.

Loss is painful, sometimes catastrophic, but like some terrible, black soil, it also has the potential to bear exquisite fruit.

But, then. *Then!* There is an upsurge of life. *What happens next?* That is the hope-filled question I am learning to ask. *What astonishingly beautiful thing happens next?*

So much happens next, but it isn't always easy. Blood, sweat, tears, time. And money. Almost always, there are bills to be paid. The dollhouse my father made for me and my sisters could be repaired with a glue gun, but dollhouses become farmhouses. What a relief, then, to remember that placemaking is always communal. "Let us make human beings in our image," God said in the beginning.[9] Like the God who made us, we are not alone in our making or our abiding. Some of us grow flowers, and some of us grow children. Some of us plant churches, and some of us plant corn. There are those of us who heal and those of us who fix. There are those of us who build. We are peacemakers. We are placemakers. We complete such small tasks, yet with each one, the whole earth moves nearer to a promised future.

The most recent repair Bill completed at Maplehurst was very small, but when it was finished, I wished I had a bottle of something sparkling to open or a handful of confetti to throw. I did not have those things because the moments most worth celebrating tend not to announce themselves on our calendars. They arrive without fanfare, and all we can do is pause. Pay attention. Stand on the lawn with our necks craned back and say, "It's finished. This one small thing is finished." Although it was a minor job, it was also the one that had crashed at my feet like a cry for help and left a screaming, black hole in the roofline above my head.

Like the God who made us, we are not alone in our making or our abiding.

Even this small job needed more than we, and more than Bill, could provide. But Bill went searching until he found a carpenter in a workshop just down the road from our hilltop. This carpenter studied the shape of Maplehurst's original roofline molding with its curves as unique as a fingerprint. He cut steel blades, called molding knives, into just the right form, and then used those knives to transform new wood into the old turning. That first handyman I had invited to Maplehurst had been right: the wooden roofline molding at Maplehurst could not be restored with an off-the-shelf product. It needed collaboration. It required a community of knowledge and skill. Now the hole in our eaves is repaired. New wood has been fitted to old, and the seam between the two has been smoothed with fresh white paint. It has been like watching a tree grow young and smooth again.

If peace is a state of harmony, if it is a kind of wholeness or completeness, then we will never find it by running away from broken things and messy places. We will find it, in truth we will make it, when we draw near to the mess with shovels and paint cans. We may have a dream of peace that looks like a country porch or an isolated mountaintop, and we may receive peace in those places, like deep breaths of fresh air, but we realize

If peace is a state of harmony, if it is a kind of wholeness or completeness, then we will never find it by running away from broken things and messy places.

our dream of peace only when we come down to that place where mountain meets valley town, country meets suburbia, city meets garden, or our past meets our present. We achieve harmony not by walling ourselves off from difficult neighbors, but by reaching out to them and opening our gates to them.

The work of wholeness and the cultivation of peace will carry us right on out and into the realm of chaos. It will lead us to edges—in the land, in our hearts, in our memories. How frightened we will sometimes be. How hopeless we will sometimes feel. And yet here is where we will make gardens. Here we will eat the fruit of them. And when joy comes in the morning, as joy always does come, we will clap our hands with all the trees of the field.

Acknowledgments

We make places in community, and we make books in community, too. I am grateful to have walked with so many in the living of this story and in the telling of it.

First, the book.

Thank you to my agent Bill Jensen and my editor Carolyn McCready. Your faithful support is everything. Thank you to the Collegeville Institute and especially Michael McGregor for the quiet place and wise advice I needed in order to begin this project well.

Thank you to Andi Ashworth, Jenni Simmons, Jennifer Strange, and the whole community of readers and contributors at Art House America, where early versions of portions of this work first appeared.

Thank you to Cameron Lawrence and Jamie Hughes for publishing a piece about trees and the gospel that I would later revise for this book. You have not only refined my stories for *In Touch Magazine,* you have helped refine me as a writer.

Thank you to Laura Brown and Elrena Evans for attending to my manuscript with heart and mind.

Thank you to Lisa-Jo Baker, Kimberly Coyle, Allison Duncan, and Amy Knorr for believing in this book when it was only a small seed.

Second, the place.

Thank you to Bill Smith, John Lindtner, and Kelly Cardwell. Your knowledge, skill, and deep love for old homes inspire me.

Thank you to my sister, Kelli Campbell, and my nephews and nieces, Tristan, Kenna, Kate, and Donovan. Maplehurst is your home, too.

Most of all, I thank my husband Jonathan and my children Lillian, Thaddeus, Beau, and Elsa. I love home for many reasons, but I love it especially because you are here.

Notes

Introduction
1. Isaiah 55:12
2. Romans 8:22

Chapter 1
1. Isaiah 30:21

Chapter 2
1. Michael Dirr, *Dirr's Encyclopedia of Trees and Shrubs* (Portland: Timber Press, 2011), 49.
2. Donald Culross Peattie, *A Natural History of North American Trees* (San Antonio: Trinity University Press, 2013), 197.
3. Ibid.
4. Gina Ingoglia, *The Tree Book: For Kids and Their Grown-ups* (Brooklyn Botanic Garden, 2008), 60.
5. Peter Wohlleben, *The Hidden Life of Trees: What They Feel, How They Communicate* (Berkeley: Greystone Books, 2015), 20.
6. Ibid., 29.
7. Ibid., 30.
8. Proverbs 30:15–16

Chapter 3
1. Richard Wilbur, "The Beautiful Changes," *Collected Poems 1943–2004* (San Diego: Harcourt, 2004).

2. Peter Wohlleben, *The Hidden Life of Trees: What They Feel, How They Communicate* (Berkeley: Greystone Books, 2015), 138.

3. Jane E. Boyd and Joseph Rucker, "No Ill Nature: The Surprising History and Science of Poison Ivy and Its Relatives," *Distillations*, Summer 2013.

4. L. H. Ziska, R. C. Sicher, K. George, and J. E. Mohan, "Rising Atmospheric Carbon Dioxide and Potential Impacts on the Growth and Toxicity of Poison Ivy," *Weed Science Society of America*, Vol. 66, Issue 3, May-June 2018, http://www.bioone .org/doi/abs/10.1614/WS-06-190?journalCode=wees.

5. Isaiah 41:17–19

Chapter 4

1. Rosemary Barrett, *Magnolias* (Buffalo, NY: Firefly Books, 2002), 12.

2. Elizabeth Bishop, "One Art," *The Complete Poems 1927–1979* (New York: Farrar, Straus and Giroux, 1983), 178.

3. Peter Wohlleben, *The Hidden Life of Trees: What They Feel, How They Communicate* (Berkeley: Greystone Books, 2015), 1–5.

4. Dana Gioia, "Words," *Interrogation at Noon* (Minneapolis: Graywolf Press, 2001), 3.

5. Michael Dirr, *Dirr's Encyclopedia of Trees and Shrubs* (Portland: Timber Press, 2011), 327.

Chapter 5

1. Halfred W. Wertz and M. Joy Callender, eds., *Penn's Woods 1682–1982* (Wayne, PA: Haverford House, 1981), 33.

2. James B. Patrick, ed., *The Heritage of Longwood Gardens: Pierre S. du Pont and His Legacy*, 2nd ed. (Little Compton, RI: Fort Church Publishers, 2008), 2.

3. Ibid., 5.

4. Ibid., 6.

5. Du Pont spend $50,083, which, in 2016, would have amounted to nearly $800,000.

6. Patrick, 6.

7. Robert Turner to William Penn, 3 August 1685, National Humanities Center, 2006, http://nationalhumanitiescenter.org/pds/amerbegin/permanence/text2/TurnerPhiladelphia.pdf.

8. W. Barksdale Maynard, *The Brandywine: An Intimate Portrait* (Philadelphia: University of Pennsylvania Press, 2015), 30.

9. Ibid., 125.

10. Harold Bruce, *Winterthur in Bloom* (Columbus, OH: Charles E. Merrill Publishing Co., 1968), 8.

11. Patrick, 12

12. Maurice Hershenson, ed., *The Moon Illusion* (Psychology Press, 1989).

Chapter 6

1. Gordon G. Whitney, *From Coastal Wilderness to Fruited Plain: A History of Environmental Change in Temperate North America from 1500 to the Present* (Cambridge: Cambridge University Press, 1996), 53.

2. F. Scott Fitzgerald, *The Great Gatsby* (New York: Scribner, 1925), 179–180.

3. Ibid.

4. Proverbs 13:12

5. Psalm 37:3–4

6. Proverbs 13:12

Chapter 7

1. David Douglas, *Wilderness Sojourn: Notes in the Desert Silence* (San Francisco: Harper & Row, 1987), 88.

2. Ibid., 4.

3. Halfred W. Wertz and M. Joy Callender, eds., *Penn's Woods 1682–1982* (Wayne, PA: Haverford House, 1981), 35.

4. Edward O. Wilson, *Biophilia* (Cambridge: Harvard University Press, 1984), 106.

Chapter 8

1. Michael Dirr, *Dirr's Encyclopedia of Trees and Shrubs* (Portland: Timber Press, 2011), 418.

2. Max Bloomfield, *Bloomfield's Illustrated Historical Guide: Embracing an Account of the Antiquities of St. Augustine, Florida* (St. Augustine: Max Bloomfield, 1885), 17.

3. Psalm 6:3

4. Eric Rutkow, *American Canopy: Trees, Forests, and the Making of a Nation* (New York: Scribner, 2012), 213.

5. Ibid.

6. Ibid., 218.

7. W. Barksdale Maynard, *The Brandywine: An Intimate Portrait* (Philadelphia: University of Pennsylvania Press, 2015), 150.

8. Psalm 22:27

Chapter 9

1. David George Haskell, *The Songs of Trees: Stories from Nature's Great Connectors* (New York: Viking, 2017), 83.

2. Michael Pollan, *Cooked: A Natural History of Transformation* (New York: Penguin Press, 2013), 311.

3. Lamentations 4:22

4. Revelation 22:2

5. 1 Chronicles 16:33; Psalm 96:12; Psalm 148:9, 13; Isaiah 55:12

6. Isaiah 51:6

7. Adele Calhoun, *Spiritual Disciplines Handbook: Practices That Transform Us* (Westmont, IL: InterVarsity Press, 2015), 9.

8. Romans 1:20

9. Isaiah 66:22

10. George Meredith, *The Poetical Works of George Meredith* (New York: Scribner, 1912), 177.

Chapter 10

1. Proverbs 29:18 KJV

2. C. S. Lewis, *The Lion, the Witch and the Wardrobe* (New York: Harper Trophy, 1950), 82.

3. C. S. Lewis, *Prince Caspian* (New York: Harper Trophy, 1951), 227.

4. Quoted in: Eric Rutkow, *American Canopy: Trees, Forests, and the Making of a Nation* (New York: Scribner, 2012), 58.

5. Eric Rutkow, *American Canopy: Trees, Forests, and the Making of a Nation* (New York: Scribner, 2012), 58.

6. Esme Raji Codell, *Seed by Seed: The Legend and Legacy of John "Appleseed" Chapman* (New York: Greenwillow Books, 2012), 11.

7. Zechariah 3:10

Chapter 11

1. Andy Crouch, *Culture Making: Recovering Our Creative Calling* (Downers Grove, IL: InterVarsity Press, 2008), 22.

2. Thomas Christopher, *In Search of Lost Roses* (Chicago: University of Chicago Press, 2002).

3. G. Michael Shoup, *Empress of the Garden* (College Station, TX: Texas A&M University Press, 2013), 62.

4. John H. Ewing and R. Scott Steele, *West Grove: A Pictorial History* (West Grove, PA, 1993), 3.

5. Katharine S. White, *Onward and Upward in the Garden* (New York: Farrar, Straus and Giroux, 1979), 76.

6. Isaiah 43:2

7. Psalm 77:16, 19

8. Peter Beales, *Passion for Roses* (New York: Rizzoli, 2005), 121.

9. Jennifer Potter, *The Rose* (London: Atlantic Books, 2010), 388.

10. Ibid.

11. Michael Dirr, *Dirr's Encyclopedia of Trees and Shrubs* (Portland: Timber Press, 2011), 8.

12. Joseph S. Illick, *Common Trees of New York* (Washington D.C.: American Tree Association, 1927), 71.

13. "Oak," Arbor Day Foundation, https://www.arborday.org/programs/nationaltree/oak.cfm.

Chapter 12

1. Michael Dirr, *Dirr's Encyclopedia of Trees and Shrubs* (Portland: Timber Press, 2011), 669.

2. Matthew Halverson, "Bernie O'Brien's Tree Sanctuary," *Southwest: The Magazine*, November 2017, https://www.south westmag.com/bernie-obriens-tree-sanctuary/.

3. John H. Ewing and R. Scott Steele, *West Grove: A Pictorial History* (West Grove, PA, 1993), 71.

4. Ibid., 5.

5. "Paul Cornell-Founder of Hyde Park," Hyde Park Historical Society, http://www.hydeparkhistory.org/2015/04/23/paul -cornell-founder-of-hyde-park/.

6. "History of Chicago's Park," Chicago Park District, https://www .chicagoparkdistrict.com/about-us/history-chicagos-park.

7. Acts 3:21

8. Nehemiah 1:9

9. Genesis 1:26 NLT